Madame Medium

Unleash Your Inner Psychic with a French Teacher Turned Psychic Medium

BETH PARKER

Copyright © 2019 Beth Parker

All rights reserved.

ISBN: 9781094830056

DEDICATION

This book is dedicated to my parents, Jim and Norene Parker, my daughters, Ann and Meg, my husband, Scott, my Spirit Guides, and all of my fabulous former students. Each of you had a hand in making me the teacher and medium I am today.

CONTENTS

	Acknowledgments	i
1	Back to School Night: *Meet the Teacher*	1
2	Confidence vs. Ego: *Believe and Receive without Getting Cocky*	14
3	Coincidence and Synchronicity: *It's a Sign… Isn't It?*	21
4	How It Works: *Spiritnet and the Clairs*	27
5	The Good, The Bad and The Ugly: *Who's Who in The Spirit World*	41
6	Intangible Protection: *The Power of Prayer*	65
7	Tangible Protection *Holy Water, Sage and Talismans, Oh My!*	72
8	Spirits and Spirits Don't Mix: *An Important Psychic P.S.A.*	75
9	Auras 101: *Understanding External Energy Fields*	79
10	Chakras 101: *Understanding Internal Energy Centers*	82

11	As the Wheel Turns: *Checking and Balancing Your Chakras*	95
12	Energy Boosting and Balancing: *Spiritual Health Habits*	101
13	Automatic Writing 101: *Get Your John Nash On*	120
14	Crystals 101: *School of Rocks*	124
15	Tarot 101: *Divination Tools for Beginners*	133
16	Psychic Circles and Partner Activities: *Sometimes More Is Merrier*	143
17	Relationships: *Another Psychic P.S.A.*	154
18	Bumps in the Road: *Managing Mindset and Expectations*	158
19	What Comes Next: *Continuing Your Educational Journey*	164

ACKNOWLEDGMENTS

Without the patience, support and love of my husband, Scott, this book would not have been possible.
You not only opened your home to me and my dog, but to countless "unexpected house guests" since.
Thank you for accepting our new reality and believing in me —and in all of my abilities— every step of the way.

Much love and many thanks to my daughter, Ann, and son-in-law, Shaun, who not only blessed me with the perfect grandchild, but also offered superb editing and technical support as I struggled to get this book published on my own.

More love and big hugs to my daughter, Meg, and son-in-law-to-be, Joe, who share my passion for all things New Age.
Thanks for making me feel "normal" and for cheering me on every step of the way.

Shout out to Kelly Lockwood of Kelalo Designs who took my cover ideas and turned them into a reality that was even better than I imagined. You rock!

PART I:

PREPARING FOR YOUR JOURNEY

A MEDIUM'S GUIDE TO THE UNIVERSE

1 BACK TO SCHOOL NIGHT

Meet the Teacher

Raise your hand if, when you first glanced at the title of this book, you thought it must be about the lady boss of a ring of high paid psychic prostitutes. Sorry to burst your bubble (and drag your mind out of the gutter), but I am just your average high school French teacher turned psychic medium hoping to help you experience some of the untapped magic that exists in the Universe for yourself. Long before I went by the title, "Medium," I was known to thousands of students as simply "Madame". I have had a couple of other nicknames as well, thanks to my best friend, Michelle, who is not only a Spanish teacher, but an avid creator of urban legends. She either calls me "DeLise" (my first married last name), or "Bruja" (the Spanish word for witch). She uses the former because she claims she "can't keep up with all of my husbands"; the latter because she swears that I was always appearing out of thin air in her classroom, scaring the bejeezus out of her. For the record, there have only been two other husbands, one of whom lasted nearly twenty years, thank you very much. As for

Bruja, although most might consider my psychic abilities supernatural (and I do appreciate the mystique that Michelle has created surrounding me), I can assure you that my suddenly materializing in her room has nothing to do with sorcery and everything to do with her crappy peripheral vision. Many of the loyal student-subjects who called me Madame also indulged me on occasion during class by chanting my self-appointed royal nickname, "La Reine" (The Queen). Unless they follow me on social media, however, they probably won't recognize me by my nom de plume, Beth Parker. Although I changed my last name legally after marrying my husband, I decided to use my maiden name professionally for two reasons. First and foremost, though no one on either side claims responsibility for my psychic DNA, my father always believed in me; as a child-artist, a mother, a teacher, and, just before he died, as a budding psychic medium. He told me (and anyone who would listen) that I was one of the smartest people he knew and that I could do anything. The second reason is more practical in nature. Though less exotic or gypsy-like than my new married name, Parker is much easier to spell and pronounce than the hot mess of consonants and vowels that my husband has been saddled with since birth, Wieczynski.

Whoever coined the phrase, "It's never too late to be who you want to be," clearly had the likes of me in mind. As someone who spent about a decade as a stay-at-home mom, nearly two decades as a high school teacher, and over three decades reading Tarot cards before embarking on a third career as a psychic medium, it goes without saying that I believe in the ability to reinvent oneself. You may consider me a late bloomer —or perhaps a slow learner— given how long it took me to recognize my gift. Whatever you consider me, the takeaway here is that if it can happen to a middle-aged twice-divorced soccer mom turned high school teacher, it can happen to you, too. I used to watch the psychic shows on television and think, "That is so cool... Why can't that be me? I wonder what Kim, Theresa or Tyler did to deserve my dream job?" Then one day it started happening to me and —once I became completely convinced that I wasn't just hearing things or hadn't lost my mind— I embraced my newfound superpowers and never looked back.

Why didn't I start hearing from the Spirit World until later in life? I attribute this to fear, timing and a not-so-little thing called Soul Purpose. If anyone had told me when I was a kid that I would one day be talking to dead people for a living, I would have pulled back the covers that I was hiding under and told them they were crazy. I spent the first decade of my life sleeping with the closet doors closed, the hall light on, and my brother in my room as often as I could con or bribe him into it. I never *ever* opened my eyes when I sensed a presence at night in my room, which would explain why I never actually *saw* dead people back in the day. If my brother wasn't there, I would keep my eyes squeezed tightly shut and silently bargain with The Others that I knew were in the room. If this tactic didn't seem to be working, I would run like a maniac into my parents' room and spend the rest of the night there. So, no, I have not been talking to the dead since I was three or seven or nine, because if they *had* managed to communicate with me in my hiding place beneath the covers, or *had* caught me in the hallway as I fled into my parents' room, I am one thousand percent certain that I would have dropped dead from fright and joined them in the Afterlife right then and there. How did I eventually become unafraid enough to do what I do now? It was definitely a gradual process, but I think it's safe to say that the seventeen years I spent teaching hormonal teenagers made me immune to most of the horrors in this life *and* the next.

I believe I can also attribute the later-than-usual onset of my psychic abilities to my first Soul Purpose in this life, motherhood. I always knew that I would be married and have children, and I did so in my early twenties, which was a bit younger than most of my peers who were busy pursuing careers back in the early 90's. I loved (and still love) being a mom to my two amazing daughters, but I don't think I would have done as good of a job had I been inundated with Spirit voices while I was raising them. I had a lot to learn about relationships as well, and I do not think that it is a coincidence that my awakening took place just as my youngest was leaving the nest and I met my husband, Scott. He is the one human who can calm my crazy and who has made me feel safe, secure and protected every single day since we met. If you get anything at all from this book and happen to meet him, please thank him. Without his open-minded acceptance of me and my unorthodox new reality, I promise you none of this would have been possible. I'd had a lot of kooky stuff happen to me at home and in my classroom in the years between hiding from The Others and meeting the love of my life on eHarmony, but it wasn't until I met Scott and his resident house ghost that my journey as a psychic medium began.

Spirits require energy to make their presence known, which is why your lights may flicker strangely or the TV may go off and on when they are trying to get your attention. As soon as

I started staying at Scott's house, I sensed that someone or *something* was trying to get my attention, big time. I've always had problems with technology and electronics acting wonky or shorting out, but this was different. There were plumbing issues; the shower, which for *months* had never gotten hot enough for me, suddenly went from lukewarm to scalding mid-shower, but only when *I* used it. The DVD player stopped working, but only when *I* was in the room. The radio station got staticky, but only when *I* entered the room. Light bulbs blew and the ceiling fixtures in the kitchen or Scott's office would flash or visibly shake, but only when *I* stood under them. Then clothing and jewelry items would go missing, but only *my* clothing and jewelry —to the point where my girlfriends and I had deduced that Scott was either secretly a cross-dresser (doubtful because even if he were, he's a foot taller and 100 lbs. heavier, so he'd never fit into my stuff)— or he had a size two sex slave chained to a radiator somewhere in the cellar. I did a thorough search of the basement and, finding no one being held captive (nor any trace of a crime scene), I began to wonder if someone or something did not want me in the house. Could it be a former resident? Scott informed me that he had bought the house from an elderly widow. The house was built circa 1950 and they had been the only previous owners. "Maybe it's the dead husband," I said. One day, when the DVD player refused to cooperate for the umpteenth time, I randomly said aloud, "Oh, for the love of God, Joe, would you please stop messing with us? It's still your house and I'm not trying to take it over!?" With a look of total shock, Scott asked, "Why did you call him Joe?" I said that I had no idea why, but I would like to watch a damn movie in peace. He shared that he had never met the man, but he remembered the old lady's name and he was pretty sure that his name had in fact been Joe. Later, he found some old paperwork with both of their names on it and there it was in plain ink: Joseph. So that was *something*. What happened a few months later was something else.

It was the day before Scott's family was coming over to celebrate his birthday. As I lay in bed thinking about what all I had to get done before they arrived, I heard someone say, "Tell Chrissy I'm fine. Tell her the name Ellen and she'll know it's me." I sat up, looked around and, seeing no one in the room with us, shook Scott and said, "Babe, did you just hear that?"

"Hear what?" was his response.

"I think it was Chrissy's mom. What was her name?" (Chrissy's mother had passed away before I met Scott and I didn't know anything about her yet.)

"Barb."

"Huh", I said, "Well this is what I just heard… I'm going to ask her about it tomorrow because I may be going crazy."

The next evening after we finished dinner, I told Chrissy what had happened (what I'd heard) and she burst into tears. I looked over at her brother, Ryan, for some explanation and he said, "Ellen was mom's middle name." When Chrissy was calm again, she added, "It's not just that… Ellen was our favorite show to watch together and as I watched it the other day I spoke to my mom and said 'I really miss watching Ellen with you… and isn't it weird how your middle name was Ellen?'" To say that we were all freaked out is an understatement, but I still thought it must be something about the house or Joseph. I mean, how could I *suddenly* start communicating with the dead at this age? Believe me, I was the biggest skeptic of all… until it started happening more frequently, and with greater depth and detail. Now my communications with Spirit last anywhere from a few moments to over an hour, depending upon the situation and how much energy each party can muster for the occasion.

Within days of Chrissy's mom communicating with me, my dad was diagnosed with lung cancer and began chemotherapy and radiation. I was, of course, sad and frightened but felt very lucky because this had occurred over the summer and as a teacher that meant I was free to go to his appointments with him. My brother and mother were there every day as well, which made it feel a bit like the good old days. Over the course of his treatment I began to not only *hear* things but *see* and communicate with members of Scott's family and my own. I kept my dad posted as my visits with the those on the Other Side progressed and he never once questioned them or doubted me. One day in September, about a week after he had finished his treatment and school had started back, I stopped over to see him and both of his deceased parents (my grandparents) joined us in Spirit. I excitedly shared their message and he confirmed all of the random details that they had shown me from his childhood that I had never known. He passed away in his sleep two nights later, somewhat unexpectedly despite the cancer. I spent the next day with him as we waited for his body to be taken away. That night I stayed with my mom, on his side of the bed, until my grandmother and aunt arrived from Michigan. Sometime after my mom fell asleep, I heard a loud, crazy frequency coming from the nightstand. It continued, but my mom never stirred. Not understanding how she was sleeping through it, but not wanting to wake her, I got up in the dark to figure it out. As soon as I reached out and felt his hearing aid, it stopped. I knew then that it was his way of checking in and letting me know that he knew I was there and that he was okay. This, of course, gave me great comfort, as did knowing that because of what I had seen and shared with him two nights before, he had passed away knowing that my grandparents would be there waiting for him. Though I grieved just as everyone does, I recognized that my new abilities had made his passing and my acceptance of it so much easier than it is for most people. I decided then that I would fully embrace this gift I had only begun to recognize and do everything I could to help others who are grieving to heal as I had.

Why do I believe I can help *you* tune into the universe and unleash your inner psychic or, at the very least, hone your intuition and experience some of the hidden wonders of the Universe? First and foremost, because of my many years of experience as a classroom teacher. Second, because I am a self-taught psychic and managed to catapult myself from clueless newbie to professional psychic medium in a relatively short period of time without ever leaving the comfort of my own home. An enthusiastic (and slightly spastic) DIY-er by nature, rather than pausing to wonder, "Why me? Why now? I said, "Hell Yes!" to the psychic medium dress and began reading and watching everything psychic-related that I could get my hands and eyes on. My enthusiasm and dedication paid off. Within the space of two years, I had sharpened my skills to the point where I was able to quit my day job and devote myself full-time to serving the Spirit World. Remember that New Age buzz word, Soul Purpose, that I mentioned earlier? I can tell you without hesitation that another one of my Soul Purposes during this go-round on Earth is to teach. I loved teaching and would have happily gone on doing so for another ten years or more had the Spirit World not come knocking on my door. The best part for me was the daily interaction with my students and knowing that I was making an impact on their lives that went beyond any French, Spanish or Italian vocabulary list or verb conjugation that came out of a textbook. Nothing, however, not even the honor of winning 2015 Senior Teacher of the Year, can compare to the sense of fulfillment that I get from connecting people with their loved ones who have passed on. Witnessing the transformation that occurs as they experience all of the validations which lead to the sense of peace that comes with the absolute knowledge that there is life and love after death brings a feeling of joy that words cannot begin to describe. Before I gave up my teaching career to serve the Spirit World full-time, I made a pact or "contract" with The Universe via my trusted Spirit Guides; they would see to it that I made as much money as I had as a teacher, and I would use what I had learned as an educator to instruct others in the how-to of my new domain. This book is just one part of the effort that I continue to make to keep up my end of the bargain.

Although I was pretty oblivious to my gifts for the first forty-plus years of my existence, as I said, lots of freaky things did happen to me before I realized I was a full-on psychic and could talk to dead people. I had dreams that predicted future events and I knew when my friends were pregnant before they knew it themselves; I knew when my parents were sick and I could feel their illness although they were miles, or states, away; I sensed that I wasn't ever really alone in the house… you get the general picture. If you are reading this, chances are better than average that you have experienced similar unexplainable things and would like to understand them, or perhaps you want to come out from under your own protective covers and take on more of these experiences yourself.

Like the wide variety of clients who come to me for psychic tutoring, not everyone who is reading this is hoping to become a professional psychic or a psychic medium. Some of you are just trying to figure out the weird stuff that has happened to you, while others are interested in learning how to tune in and connect with your Guides in order to figure out why or how to make better use of the intuitive gifts we are all born with. You may find that developing these gifts assists you in your current career in the medical field or law enforcement (most people in these fields already have sharper than average intuition, by the way). Likewise, not everyone reading this is at the same level on the development continuum. Some of you may already have connected with your Guides and are looking for a bit of clarification, but the vast majority are probably still scratching your heads and wondering why you wake up at 3:33 every morning with a random song stuck in your head. Whatever your reasons may be, I feel confident that the lessons and assignments provided here will help you on your journey to becoming more awakened and aware in this life.

When I say that I can help you to unleash your inner psychic, this does not mean that you will read this book and walk away ready to schedule readings for fifty or one-hundred bucks an hour. Just as everyone is born with *some* mathematical aptitude, we are all born with *some* level of intuitive awareness. Just as with math, however, we may need a little help getting beyond the basics. This is why we have teachers and textbooks. I had the fabulous Mr. Sheridan and his tomes to get me through Geometry and Trigonometry, and you now have me and this book to help explain the world of intuitives, psychics and mediums. While I can introduce and explain many tools and tricks that will lead you to heightened intuition and attunement, I cannot *make* you psychic or more psychic. I cannot guarantee that reading this book will lead to a career as an intuitive life coach, professional psychic or psychic medium. I *can* help you to understand how it all works and give you a starting point based on my own experiences. How far you go, or what level you get to, is entirely up to you and the Universe. It may seem as if I took myself from point A to point Z overnight, but I was 110% dedicated and it took a ton of work on my end. It sometimes seems incredible, even to me, how far I got in such a short time... until I think back and calculate just how many hours I devoted to my new craft. I essentially had two full-time jobs the last two years of my teaching career. I read a quote recently —I can't remember where I found it, so forgive me for not giving the author credit— that said something to the effect of, "Six months of consistent grinding will put you two years ahead with your goals." While I am quick to give most of the credit to God and my Guides, make no mistake, I spent those two years grinding. I devoted roughly two hours every morning to prayer, meditation and dictating messages from the Spirit World. I would wake up at the butt crack of dawn (4:00 am) and do Spirit Work until 6:00 am, when I had to get ready for school each day. When you add those hours up, I spent roughly 720 hours over two school years just on my morning work. Add another two hours (at the very least) per day after school and six hours per day (another low-ball estimate) during the summer breaks. All of these hours were spent reading, learning and delivering hundreds of messages, either on the spot or via one of my sparkly notebooks that I filled during my morning sessions with Spirit.

All told, it adds up to about 1,680 hours total, or 42 straight 40-hour-weeks of grinding. This figure does not include weekends and holidays, which I rarely took off. So, while I have no formal degree in mediumship, I think it is safe to say I have earned an honorary PhD in my fifth language, which I call Spirit Speak. Bottom line: I guarantee that you will get *something* out of this book but, I must again stress that how much you get out of it depends on how much you are willing to put into it.

One last word of warning before you undertake the next steps in launching your psychic superpowers. If your intention in developing your intuition or honing your psychic skills is based on monetary gain or the ability to control others in some way, you may as well stop reading and hang it up right now, because it ain't gonna happen. If you are just looking to be nosy or think it would be cool to sneak a peek into people's private lives, you're wasting your time. The thought of reading someone else's diary makes me cringe and there are things I wish I could un-see after a reading. I am also way over having any drama in my life and do my best not to invite any in from either side of the veil. Anything falling under the category of "juicy tidbits" are provided if —and only if— they can be used to help or protect someone in some way, not just for the sake of my or anyone else's curiosity. In short, the information you receive from Above will be doled out on a need-to-know basis. I was shown the winners of *Survivor* and *Dancing with the Stars* before they were announced one season early on in my development, but that was for learning purposes only —to illustrate what my Guides were capable of— and hasn't happened since. So, take a deep breath and accept the fact that you'll probably have to wait until the season finale of *Game of*

Thrones just like the rest of the non-psychic world to find out if everyone's favorite hottie, Jon Snow, lays claim the Iron Throne. You won't be privy to the winning lotto numbers either because, be honest, if you did, you might just go on a massive shopping spree or coke binge and stop serving Spirit altogether, which is the whole point of being psychic. You *must* be in it for the greater good with your priority being to benefit others more than yourself. If this is the case —and you do solemnly swear to use any newfound powers for good rather than evil— please read on and take full advantage of the tutoring offered here, which should get you started on the path to tuning into the Universal Higher Power that is always working toward our collective destiny and raising consciousness.

2 CONFIDENCE VS. EGO

Believe and Receive without Getting Cocky

As a teacher I knew instinctively that the only way to get my students to buy into what I was teaching was to believe in myself enough to get them on board, and I somehow managed to get them on board with some pretty crazy schemes. One such scheme involved a tween mannequin that I dressed up in our school colors and dragged around everywhere taking pictures in the name of boosting school spirit. You may laugh, but at one point, Sapphire (aka "Gator Girl") had her own Instagram account with more followers than many of my students had. The other bandwagon I got most of them to climb aboard involved a French snow cult. The one useful (and fun!) predictive psychic ability that I enjoyed —without being aware of exactly how I was doing it— involved one of my favorite things in the whole world while I was teaching... SNOW DAYS! It's no secret to anyone whom I have taught or taught with that I created a snow cult in my classroom that functioned —successfully I might add— for about a decade. If I sensed true potential for a snow day or delay, we would chant to our own "Dieu de la Neige" (a papier-mâché Snow God) in French, in the hopes of getting a day off. I didn't keep a close tally, but I would guesstimate that our accuracy rate was well above eighty percent. The year that I won Senior Teacher of the Year and was asked to speak at graduation, I apologized to the County Superintendent of Schools for the ridiculous number of snow days that we may or may not have been responsible for during the previous four years. The moral of this little story is that while our success rate may have had something to do with my unknown psychic abilities, I suspect it that it had just as much to do with the credo, "If ya wanna receive, ya gotta believe." Some might argue that global warming was behind our leaner years in terms of snow days, but I attribute it to a less zealous group of French students on the third floor and the role that absolute belief plays in overcoming any and all obstacles that we may face. For the moment, don't stress about whether or not your future involves a career predicting snow days or reuniting people with their loved ones from the front seat of an Uber, à la Thomas John, alias *Seatbelt Psychic*. For now, please just focus on believing in yourself and in your ability to open up to whatever the Universe has in store for you as you begin to connect in a way that allows you to experience a world beyond that which you can touch, see or hear. If you are meant to be a medium, there will be no escaping the dead. They will find *and follow* you to the dry cleaners, to Starbucks and wherever else you may go, trust me on this. Then trust in yourself and your Guides to determine the rest.

In Luis Garcia's, *The Law of Ambition*, he writes, "Slow success builds character. Fast success builds ego." I couldn't agree more. Work hard and be proud of any progress that you make, no matter how long it takes. There is a fine line between confident and cocky and, as a psychic or medium, you must have enough ego to deal with the skeptics and haters but not so much that it becomes all about *you* rather than the greater good. Do not waste your time worrying whether or not you have crossed the line between appreciation and arrogance, because I can assure you that, like any good parent, the Universe will step in and slow your roll very quickly if that is indeed the case. As I explained earlier, when I quit teaching to become a full-time professional psychic medium, I didn't ask Spirit to make me rich or famous, just that I make as much as I had as a teacher. This was a rather reasonable request in my estimation, and within a few months, Spirit kept up their end of the bargain and I was starting to book up a few weeks in advance. It was clearly too much too soon however, because the Universe let me know I was being a little too picky about how I chose to use my gift and put the brakes on my bookings just long enough for me to reflect on who is driving the Magic School Bus that I am lucky enough to ride on. This little hiatus in activity (and funds) made me supremely grateful for *every* opportunity that came my way afterward. It's natural to be proud of your achievements, those little victories in the form of validations that you receive as you are honing your psychic skills, but always remember that you wouldn't be doing any of it without the help of God, the Angels, your trusted Guides, and the Universe. I do my best to take little or no credit whenever possible. When someone says, "Thank you. OMG. You're amazing," I am quick] to point out that it isn't *me*, I'm just a human antenna who is fortunate enough to play metaphysical messenger. I ask them to thank everyone on the Other Side who is working their butt off to communicate through a spaz like me!

Time to talk about another buzz word you've probably heard a time or ten... mindset. The mindset that needs to be addressed here is how you perceive and feel about yourself. Remember the little train that could? I have always had a can-do attitude toward any challenge or task, and the same was true when I began communicating with Spirit. This positive attitude is largely thanks to having been raised by loving parents who taught me to believe in myself. I was also fortunate enough to have been surrounded by many other supportive friends and family members during the developmental stages of my new career, several of whom didn't have much choice in the matter. My daughters and best friends at school became my on-the-spot guinea pigs and sounding boards, helping me to sort out what worked or didn't work as I was decoding the signs and symbols that Spirit sent me. I would announce that my head was tingling, all conversation would stop and all eyes —some nervous like a deer in the headlights— would be on me as they waited to see who my latest download from Spiritnet would be for. Others, like my then boyfriend (now husband) could easily have cut and run. Rather than being totally weirded out by what began happening in his house upon my arrival, however, he jumped right on board the crazy train and gave me the same unconditional love and support that my parents had always given me. This was a double blessing from the Universe, coming at a time when I was experiencing some of the most magical moments of my life as I recognized my gift, as well as the most difficult, involving the unexpectedly quick loss of my father to cancer and the rapid decline of my mother to the ravages of early-onset Alzheimer's.

Whether or not you are surrounded by the best of the best as I was, or a bunch of jaded and fearful skeptics, you *must* learn to trust yourself and your intuition as you begin seeing, hearing and sensing things that others around you are, for the most part, completely unaware of. A healthy dose of self-confidence is necessary as you begin to navigate the oft tricky waters of the Spirit World. Fortunately, this gets easier the more you tune in and the "hits" and validations become too great to ignore but, trust me, if you don't believe in yourself at the outset, no one else will either. Years ago, I came to the conclusion that there are two main factors that affect just about every aspect of our lives: control and confidence. I call them "The Two C's" and often find myself explaining how powerful they are and how important it is to get a handle on them in order to function as a balanced and loving individual. The world is full of control freaks. I'm sure you know at least a few, and Lord knows I do because the teaching profession has more than its fair share of them. You know who I'm talking about. The teachers who take themselves and their subject *way* too seriously and have decided that they "don't give A's", based on some unexplained (and totally whack) principle. These same teachers have usually convinced themselves and Tiger Moms everywhere that three hours of AP History homework somehow makes them a better teacher or will perhaps make their Tiger Cub a better person. You may not have had any control over them —and I'm here to tell you that as a psychic or medium you often have very little control over what you receive from the Spirit World— but you do have control over yourself and your own mindset. A good medium will do their best to interview whomever they are communicating with and help direct the conversation, but it is ultimately up to Spirit to decide what is shared. You can ask whatever you want (or whatever the client would like you to ask), but there is simply no guarantee that they will answer it. I have to remind clients of this fact, as well as the fact that I don't have the answer to every question in the Universe at my fingertips. Some of the secrets of the Universe are closely guarded and available on a need-to-know basis. If Spirit feels that you or someone else will benefit from information that is generally "password protected," they'll make you privy to it. If not, you can ask as many times as you like, but unless and until they decide the timing is right, you may as well go beat your head against the wall. Rather than being frustrated by this, I have learned to let go of the illusion that I need to be in total control during any communication with Spirit and accept each experience for what it is, a team effort.

Now on to the second C, confidence. Having too much or too little can wreak havoc on just about any relationship in your everyday life, and the same is true of your relationship with Spirit. I love Dr. Phil and often find myself quoting him. "Would you rather be right or happy?" is one of my favorite lines of his. If you have a healthy amount of confidence and ego, you will not constantly feel the need to be right, nor compelled to fight to prove your point. I'm not telling you to flatten yourself into a one-dimensional human doormat in order to avoid any and all confrontation, but the ability to agree to disagree allows us to work and play well with others. If you want to work and play well with those in the Spirit World, you need to recognize that it is not about proving your amazing gift. You're not going to like everything (or everyone) you see or hear from on the Other Side. You need to have the confidence to leave all judgment aside, sit back, and do more listening than talking because, again, it's not about you or your opinions, it's about *them* getting their message across. Focus on and have confidence in your ability to receive and deliver, and you're more likely to get that message correct. As a linguist, I am used to hearing something and mentally translating it into another language. As a medium I find it helpful to do the same. I simply play the role of interpreter, taking whatever Spirit gives me and translating it into something that the client will understand.

The next chapter is dedicated to helping you recognize and understand the signs that you may receive from the Universe or Spirit. The fact that you are reading this right now is probably no accident or coincidence. Just as my reading certain books at exactly the right time was critical to my development, so might this book be to yours. I urge you to pay close attention to all of the synchronicities and signs the Universe puts in your path and, if you are serious about honing your skills and taking them to the next level, to start taking notes. Most of the margins of the books I have read are full of scribbled notes, with important pages flagged by sticky notes and tabs. If you are holding a paper version of this book, flip to the back and you will find a few extra blank pages for your own note-taking purposes. I keep a pen or pencil handy at all times; my phone is also full of notes that I voice record when my hands are otherwise occupied, or I can't immediately lay them on a writing utensil.

3 COINCIDENCE AND SYNCHRONICITY

It's a Sign... Isn't It?

Aside from believing in yourself, one of the things that you have got to train your brain to do is to stop second-guessing or brushing off the magical synchronicities that Spirit is sending you as mere "coincidence." This is important because, unless you start paying attention to and believing in them, you will quickly find yourself stuck in neutral. We all know what a coincidence is, but what exactly is synchronicity, aside from a top ten 80's hit put out by The Police? According to Mr. Webster, it is "the coincidental occurrence of events and especially psychic events (such as similar thoughts in widely separated persons or a mental image of an unexpected event before it happens) that seem related but are not explained by conventional mechanisms of causality." In other words, synchronicities are the crazy "coincidences" that are so in your face and clearly anything but random that, unless you are the most hardheaded of skeptics, you simply cannot just chalk up to mere happenstance. These synchronicities are in fact signs from the Universe (or from our deceased loved ones) that are too obvious to be dismissed. I experience this phenomenon daily, sometimes hourly, and a large part of my job is validating the signs that Spirit has been throwing in the path of those who come to me for a reading. These synchronicities come in all shapes and sizes and are otherwise known as the things that make you go *Hmmm*.

Sometimes these synchronicities are so great that you recognize them immediately for what they are. Other times, however, they are much more subtle, and it takes a while before it hits you. I was just about clobbered over the head with one of the former in 2001, after having spent eight years as a stay-at-home mom. It was the October after 9/11 and, in addition to my full-time gig as mom and Girl Scout Leader, I also worked part-time for the family contracting business, answering phones and keeping track of the books when my snowbird parents were away at their home in Florida. My youngest daughter had just entered kindergarten and I was a bit bored and frustrated and wanted to use the language teaching degree I had received a decade before, so I decided that I would look for any job that I could find in the school system to get my foot in the door. It was a Friday. I went online and searched jobs on our county school system's website and, after what seemed like ages —this was in the days of dial up internet, when a simple search meant an excruciating wait through interminable beeps, buzzes and screeches— what appeared on the screen blew my mind. It wasn't just *any* job it was the *perfect* job: Part-Time Long-Term French and Italian Substitute Teacher. Yes, you read that correctly. French and *Italian*. Not just one, but both of the languages that I had studied in college. I dropped what I was doing, stood up, raised my hands to the heavens and declared, "I get it, God. I asked and you delivered. I'm calling the number listed NOW!" I interviewed on Monday and within a week I had started my second calling as a high school language teacher.

In case you aren't yet impressed or convinced, I'll share a few more that involve my third calling, psychic medium. These are the types of synchronicities that you may have already been experiencing or will perhaps experience for the first time as you read this book. I'll introduce you a bit more to my Main Spirit Guide later when we tackle that topic, but for now please just make a mental note of her name, which is Amanda. While not the least common first name among the English-speaking population, it is hardly at the top of the pack alongside the countless Brittanys and Ashleys of a few decades back. After I (finally!?) figured out who my Amanda was, however, that name started popping up in ways that I could not ignore. My first paying client? Amanda. The first client I had who was brave enough to come see me a mere three weeks after losing her brother? Amanda. The first awful dad joke I heard from a father on the Other Side?

Knock knock.
Who's There?
Amanda.
Amanda who?
Amanda hug and kiss.

At one point early on, before I was booked weeks or months in advance, I had *three* Amandas in the space of ten days. Coincidence? I think not. I always pay special attention anytime her name appears in my appointment book because there will inevitably be some special lesson in store for me.

I often use the next few examples of synchronicity to help those who have lost a loved one, but they are also instructive to anyone who is uncertain when it comes to trusting their instincts about the signs Spirit is sending. As a medium, I am used to seeing and accepting signs and symbols as a regular part of the language that I use when communicating with Spirit, but most people —even those who practically get slapped in the face with the same sign every day— come to me wanting or needing confirmation that what they are experiencing is in fact "a sign" from their loved ones. Trust me when I say it is no coincidence that you see robins or cardinals nearly every day from April through October, or that a butterfly literally pops out of nowhere (and flies in your face or follows you) whenever you take a walk in the summer months, or that you find the same coin over and over, or that you wake up at exactly 2:24 am every morning, which happens to have been your loved one's birthday. This *is* your loved one trying to make their presence known. To clarify, it is not actually your loved one. They haven't magically morphed into a bird or a butterfly or a dime. It is their energy manipulating the objects in your environment in a way that you will notice and hopefully appreciate. Helping Spirit validate or prove that it is most definitely them is one of the best parts of my job. Most of the time Spirit will show me an image or play me a song during your reading related to the sign or signs that they have been putting in your path. Some overachieving Spirits, however, blow even my well-trained mind before, during and sometimes even after a reading with their creativity and ingenuity.

As I said, in my crazy world, there is no such thing as a coincidence, and I have learned to pay attention to and make note of anything that the Universe throws in my path or makes sure that I see repeatedly. If my down-filled throw pillows start molting and leaving feathers everywhere, I grab one and put it in my office so I remember to mention it at my upcoming reading, because I know that the person due to show up either also has cushions that are mysteriously spewing bird fur or is finding random feathers on a regular basis. Ditto on pennies, dimes and other coins that mysteriously pop up in my laundry or on my floor just before a reading. They are never for me because, let's face it, I don't need any signs to know that your people (or mine) are present. Spirit can have a real field day with your cell phone, radio and other electronics as well. Does your car radio change stations on its own? Does your or your loved one's favorite singer or song come on just as you are thinking about them? Not a coincidence, Scout's Honor. I once had a deceased dad blurt out, "Crosby, Stills & Nash!", as a couple was preparing to leave my office. Dad had also suggested that his daughter get back into her favorite pastime, gardening. Not only had he named of one of the couple's favorite bands and his daughter's hobby of choice, but the next day when she decided to take dad's advice, guess who came on the radio just as she stuck her hands back in the dirt? Yep. Crosby, Stills & Nash.

What about animals, you ask? Spirit just loves using all manner of plants and wildlife to give you a poke. If I hear the song "Rockin' Robin", I know to ask if there is anyone named Robin in the family and, if there isn't, ten out of ten times someone has just seen a robin or another species of bird, or has been encountering an overabundance of birds that their loved ones have magically managed to put directly in their path. Butterflies, hummingbirds and dragonflies are super popular with the deceased, but I've also had a few cases of deer literally coming out of the woodwork (or up to the window) courtesy of their dearly departed. The tap-tap-tapping of little paws across your floor when you no longer have pets is a telltale sign that your pets who have passed are trying to make their presence known. You may also feel a tingling sensation or a cool breeze at your ankles (at pet-level) as you reminisce fondly about BooBoo the cat or Tootsie the dog. Both are signs. Sudden inexplicable changes in room temperature or the behavior of your living pets can also help you discern when Spirit is present. If you suspect that someone from the Spirit World is paying you a visit and your furry friends are staring in a strange way, wigging out, or flat-out refuse to enter a certain room, trust your gut. Animals are generally much more sensitive to the Spirit World than we humans are, so whether the hair stands up on the back of your neck or not, their shackles going up is often all the confirmation you need.

What might this mean for those of you who are currently grieving a loss? What does all of this synchronicity and sign stuff mean to you, the budding intuitive or psychic? If you are having similar experiences and still wondering about the origin of the things you are hearing, seeing or finding, unless you believe in the dime fairy —in which case you should definitely believe in your loved ones— there is no explanation other than the obvious: they are synchronicities, or signs.

P.S. As I was typing this, I received a text from a recent client asking about a monarch butterfly she had just seen... which I of course took as a sign!

4 HOW IT WORKS

Spiritnet and the Clairs

One of the most difficult things for me as a DIY developing medium was grasping exactly who's who in the Spirit World, and what their roles are. Just as you are reading this book, I read everything I could get my hands on to help me learn to navigate my new life between worlds. Shout-out to my personal heroes, mediums John Edward, James Van Praagh and Kim Russo for having authored books that made everything so much clearer to me as I was homeschooling myself. If you are, as I was, reading this after having had some direct contact with the Spirit World, you already know how confusing it can be trying to decipher some of the seemingly random information that you receive from the dimensions beyond what most people consider the "real world." While I can't be there to solve every riddle for you, I can give those of you with zero experience a starting point, or (fingers crossed!) clarify things for those of you who have been going at it alone and have plateaued or can't seem to get out of first or second gear. As a student I found it easiest to learn concepts when there was a story, analogy or metaphor attached. As a teacher, I always did my best to attach some meaning to whatever was in my daily lesson plan to make things easier to remember. Not surprisingly, you can expect to find a lot of analogies here, starting right now, with a few that will help me to explain the who, what, when, where and how of the Spirit World.

The first question most people ask is, "How?" As in, "How does it work?" or "How can you see, hear, feel or know these things?" To answer the *How*, I must first explain the *Where*, which is actually quite simple to do using the first of many analogies. We are all, of course, familiar with the internet, satellites and cable television. I find it easiest to think of the part of the Universe where psychics and mediums get their information as another internet or satellite network, which I call the "Spiritnet". When we say they are "tuning in," we are connecting to this second World Wide (Spirit) Web using what most people call the sixth sense. This sixth sense is actually made up of several sixth senses, also known as the "Clairs"; clairvoyance, clairaudience, clairsentience, and claircognizance. These Clairs may at first feel like four mean girls out to make your life a living hell with their bitchy little tricks, but once you understand how they work, you'll realize that they actually *totes* want everyone to be a part of their clique, using all that each of them has to offer toward the betterment of ourselves and the world at large; the end result being everyone coming together to sit at the cool table at lunch, sharing a Coke and a smile. So, who or what are these Clairs and how can you recognize them in a crowded lunchroom?

Clairvoyance (clear seeing) is the ability to see things that aren't actually tangible —that you can't reach out and touch or feel— using your mind's eye. These images or scenes are somewhat easier to identify and trust your instincts about than the manifestations of the other Clairs. They also often come on the heels of some physical sensation meant to grab your attention. You might feel a tingling, pulsing or twitching somewhere on your body and the next thing you know you are looking at what appears to be an Instagram post or a YouTube video, even though you know that you didn't consciously cue it up. My Guides, as well as the loving Spirits of the deceased that I encounter on the Other Side, use this Clair to show me famous TV characters who either, 1) represent an archetype who has something in common with them, or 2) happen to look like someone here or on the Other Side. For example, depending on which Golden Girl they show me, I know whether I am dealing with a no-nonsense female like Dorothy, a spunky little Sophia, a saucy (and perhaps promiscuous) Blanche, or someone like her naïve counterpart, Rose. Cindy from the Brady Bunch means a younger sister or step-sister; Joey from Friends indicates a male friend; George Lopez's mother lets me know I have a Latina mother or grandmother in the house... and so forth. If I see only a brief glimpse of one of these archetypes, I know that they are simply using it to describe someone, more often than not a living person. If the archetype moves and interacts with me as if we were playing charades, I know that I am communicating with someone on The Other Side. As a medium, this Clair can also help me to distinguish where someone currently resides in the Spirit World. If they are safely settled on the Other Side, they will appear to be more remote, as if on a stage in the distance. If they are "stuck" between worlds or have chosen to hang out on this plane to remain close to a beloved spouse of many years, they appear to be much closer, in the room with me, or how most ghosts and apparitions are portrayed in the media. I also sometimes see words or names spelled out rather than hearing them. If my eyelid suddenly starts twitching for no apparent reason, it means that Spirit wants to show me something, or that I need to pay close attention to something going on around me. The next time you get the same sensation, try not to dismiss it offhand or go running to the ophthalmologist. It may be that Spirit wants you to pay attention so that they can show you something. I'll go into detail about Chakras later in chapter 10, but this Clair is tied to the Third Eye Chakra, so I like to picture her as a big dark blue eye in the center of my forehead.

Clairaudience (clear hearing) is the ability to hear things that are not audible to the average listener. This was the first of the Clairs to kick-in for me. Remember the story I shared about hearing my sister-in-law's mother as I was lying in bed? It was kind of like an instant download from the Spiritnet in the form of a voice other than my own sharing information with me. Thankfully when I relayed the message the next day it made total sense, which validated that I had in fact heard from my first dead person, as opposed to having a case of midlife schizophrenia. Speaking of going mad, have you ever had a random song —one that you haven't heard in ages— start playing incessantly in your head? Yep, that's more than likely Spirit trying to send you a message via clairaudience. If I hear Queen's "Under Pressure", one more time first thing in the morning as a reminder to finish this manuscript within the next month, I may just blow a gasket. The Spirit World just loves music because it raises our vibration, which in turn makes it easier for them to communicate with us. I cannot tell you how often I hear songs during a reading, or during the course of any given day. When I do, I've learned that I damn well better take note and tune in. One day I kept hearing the Beatles' *Baby You Can Drive My Car* ad nauseum. With no readings coming up that afternoon, I ignored it and went on with my day. Big mistake. A bit later I hopped into *not* my own car, but my husband's to run an errand... and promptly backed into our neighbor's truck. You can Imagine the teasing I endured from my husband about the psychic not seeing it coming. I don't always know exactly *why* I'm hearing a particular song, but I never ignore them during readings either. If I hear *Like a Rhinestone Cowboy*, I can narrow it down to someone loving country western clothing or music, being a Glen Campbell fan, or that there's someone named Glen in the mix. It once turned out to be the first 45 record someone had bought, which is just the sort of random but an example of a specific magical memory detail that Spirit loves to pull out of their hat. As I write this there is a distinct high frequency in my left ear that only I (and maybe my dog) can hear. When this at times annoying mic-like feedback takes over, or my ear starts to pop despite the fact that my altitude has not altered in any way, I know that I am receiving direct guidance or information from Spirit. Once again, it is all too easy to assume that you've got a case of tinnitus (ringing in the ears) from cranking your car radio or headphone volume too high, when it could be Spirit tugging your ear, attempting to get you to listen up or tune in. It can also be a sign that your Throat Chakra, which is associated with clairaudience is blocked.

Clairsentience (clear feeling) is associated with both the Heart and Solar Plexus Chakras. This is the Clair that 99% of the population has experienced and can relate to on some level, but it is a bit harder to nail down in writing. It often takes the form of the instinctual "gut feelings" that we get in the center of our bodies, or the empathy or fear that tugs at our hearts in times of sadness or stress. If you are an empath, psychic or not, you naturally sense or feel not only your own emotions, but what others around you are sensing and feeling. As a result, you are far more prone to be at the mercy of this Clair. The gift of clairsentience —I hesitate to call it a gift because it can be very distressing to feel everything that is going on around you, especially in crowded places— is very useful before and during a reading, but can be a complete nuisance afterwards if you don't learn to manage any lingering energy that isn't your own. Before a client comes in I usually pick up on and feel whatever they are feeling, emotionally or physically. I suffer from migraines, but I know that Spirit would never allow me to actually get one during a reading, so if I start getting the telltale visual disturbances or pings of pain, I make a note of it so that I can share it with the person when they arrive and *voilà!*, my symptoms disappear as quickly as they arrived. If I have a true Nervous Nelly on my hands, I might get anxious to the point of nausea beforehand. During a reading the same eye twitches that tell me to pay attention during the course of the day can be an indicator that someone on this side or the other has had (or is having) problems with their vision. I've never been a big shopper, but I am even more grateful for the Power of Prime now that I can't go to Home Depot without getting a sudden backache, only to turn the corner to find someone who has pulled their back out attempting to lift something heavy in the next aisle. Many of my nurse friends have shared that they have gone a little whacky themselves at times, thinking they have the same symptoms, and therefore diseases, of those they are treating. My theory is that most nurses are empaths (who also tend to be the born caretakers among us) and can't help but pick up on what others are feeling. The lesson here is, you guessed it, to pay attention to what you are feeling and not rush to the conclusion that you have some physical issue when it might just be someone else's vibes encroaching on your personal spiritual space or energetic field. If any of this information hit you like a punch in the Solar Plexus, fear not, lots of tips and tricks for avoiding the perils of the empath await you as you read further.

I'm going to throw clear tasting (clairgustance) and clear smelling (clairscent) together here as "bonus" Clairs because they go hand-in-hand and are rather easy to explain and discern. Clairgustance is relatively rare for me, but if I suddenly get a metallic or coppery taste in my mouth without having sucked on an open wound or a some spare change, I know to ask how the person in front of me connects with that sensation, because they undoubtedly will in some way. Likewise, when I smell something that isn't actually stinking up the room or house, it is easy to validate because I simply ask whomever I am with whether they smell Aqua Velva aftershave or bacon and eggs cooking. If they do, case closed. If they don't, it usually turns out to be the scent someone wore or that breakfast was their favorite meal of the day.

Claircognizance (clear knowing) is the most likely to leave you wondering whether it is your own thought or a download from The Spiritnet. If a thought or the answer to something pops into your head seemingly out of nowhere, you are most likely dealing with claircognizance. It's that feeling you get when you *know* something but have no idea where the knowledge came from or *how* you know it. This phenomenon usually occurs for me when I'm super connected to or on the same wavelength as someone in the Spirit World. A reading will be rolling right along with images, words and whatnot flowing effortlessly and then *boom*, without hearing a voice I somehow know exactly what message they need me to pass along.

How do you know if you are receiving information via one of the Clairs, rather than it just being a figment of your imagination or, Heaven forbid, as a result of some delusional episode? The obvious answer is that whatever it is you have seen or heard or felt is immediately (or eventually) validated in the "real world." Here's an example that was shared with me by a psychic student. You are at the grocery store picking up your favorite energy drink when you suddenly *see* (in your mind's eye) your sister, who no longer lives with you, grabbing one out of the fridge, so you decide to buy two. The next day your sister stops by to visit and calls out from the kitchen, "Is it okay if I take one of these energy drinks?" Rather than being as annoyed as you normally would, you are able to respond with generosity because you paid attention to one of the Clairs and now have a spare on hand to meet your own future craving. Your Guides will find other ways of helping you to distinguish your own thoughts from information sent from them. If am receiving intuitive medical information from my Health Guide, I will hear a term like *pruritus* (the medical term for itching), which I clearly would not have heard or known without their assistance. They also help me to separate my own thoughts from the knowledge they are imparting by using words in one of the other languages that I speak. If the forecast is iffy and one of my teacher friends want to know if they'll get a snow day, I will usually get a strong "*FERMÉ!*" (closed) or "*DELAI!*" (delay) from one of my bilingual Guides in response. As a learner I am about 50/50 auditory and visual and, as a psychic, when I first began receiving messages, I was predominantly clairaudient and clairvoyant, hearing or seeing the majority of what I got from Spirit. After a while, however, clairsentience and claircognizance kicked in. I am now just as likely to experience a lot of physical sensations and/or just know things, without having heard or been shown them. Chances are you will find that one or two of the Clairs are dominant and become your BFFs from the onset as well, but that doesn't mean that the others won't add you as a friend in due time.

Now that you have a basic understanding of the Clairs and the ways in which you can expect to receive information psychically, let's get back to another aspect of *How* it all works. I speak four languages (five if you count Spirit Speak), but I can promise you that none of them is math. Thanks to a few awesome teachers, I got A's and B's without much effort all the way through Algebra and Geometry, but about the time I entered Trigonometry and heard the words sine and cosine, my brain went off on a tangent, my eyes glazed over, and I got a tutor who basically dragged me through my last year of formal mathematics. Ditto Science. Loved biology, but chemistry and physics involved way too much math, and I managed to scrape through those subjects with the help of a couple of brainy high school boyfriends who doubled as lab partners. Why am I sharing this, you ask? So that you won't be expecting a super scholarly or scientific explanation of how the Universe works here. I can solve a Rubik's Cube, but I've never won any awards at the Science Fair and there are no Stephen Hawkings in my family tree. The truth is, I know that it involves the exchange of energy, and the shows I devoured on the Gaia channel involving Quantum Physics and the magical effect of our thoughts on water made a lot of sense as I watched them, but within 24 hours or so, *POOF!*, that knowledge was banished to the same corner of my brain where sine and cosine still sit collecting dust. Because of my lack of mathematical and scientific genius, I generally give the following rather unscientific explanation. Think of your brain as a satellite TV receiver. Each of our brains comes with basic cable, which includes channels like TNT, ID, HGTV and so forth. There are two channels, CNN and ESPN, for which I have absolutely no use. Today's news is, in my opinion, either terribly depressing or ridiculously biased, and the only sports I have any interest in watching are untelevised matches being played at a local school, featuring amateur players whom I know and love. This being the case, whoever is in charge of installing the brain cable boxes before we are born decided, when I came through the line, to ditch CNN and ESPN and replace them with what I refer to as The Psychic Channel (TPC) and The Medium Channel (TMC).

These two channels link me to The Spiritnet and, with the help of the fabulous Clairs, allow me to tune into energy and knowledge that cannot be seen, heard or felt using the five basic senses which serve mankind daily on the earthly plane. From what I have read and been shown during the time I have spent with Spirit, only mediums (those who can talk to dead people) are born with both channels mentioned above, but everyone is born with The Psychic Channel (TPC), which means we all have the ability to raise our vibration, and sharpen our intuition or psychic sixth sense to some degree. If, after reading my channel analogy, you are a bit dismayed and find yourself thinking, *Oh no! That means I'm not a medium and never will be!?*, please remember, once again, that while I was born with these abilities, I did not recognize them or start hearing from the dead until the ripe old age of forty-five, so there's always a chance that you will discover that you have *both* of these channels installed, regardless of your age or lack of previous experiences. Allow me break these two channels down a bit further and clarify the difference so that, as you are developing whatever gifts the Universe has in store for you, you are able to better identify what you are receiving and from where.

All mediums are psychic, but not all psychics are mediums. If you think that sounds like a confusing logic riddle designed to test your I.Q., you aren't alone. So, what exactly is the difference between a psychic and a psychic medium (aka medium)? Here's the basic deal: psychics have the ability to gather intel about past, present and future events using one or more of the Clairs, whereas mediums are able to do that, with the added bonus of being able to communicate with those who have passed on from the physical world (i.e. talk to the dead). Here's a simple analogy: all neurosurgeons are doctors, but not all doctors are neurosurgeons. Both have the same basic skill set, but neurosurgeons are specialists. Mind you, I am not comparing myself to a doctor or a neurosurgeon, both of whom have true superpowers. You would not want me operating on your brain, nor driving your car for that matter.

Unbeknownst to me, I had been fielding general psychic information for at least thirty years prior to recognizing and developing the gift of mediumship. I say unbeknownst because most of this information came when I read tarot cards for my friends and relatives, and I was clueless about the how and why of my accurate predictions. Knowing nothing about my Guides, nor how the Spirit World works, I simply assumed it was somehow the cards "working." I also had random psychic hair dreams for years. I would dream someone had a radical hair change and then walk into the office or classroom and there they would be, sporting the new 'do! I actually used to lament the fact that I possessed such a "useless psychic power." My journey into mediumship did not begin until much later and it was much more obvious to me what was happening because, from the onset, all of my experiences involved direct communication with the deceased family members and friends of people I knew. My head would tingle, I would see someone that I knew (either the deceased or, if I had never met the deceased, the person for whom the message was intended), and then the "conversation" would begin. It took me a while to figure out that not all of the information that I was getting during a reading was from your people in the Spirit World, but from my own trusted Guides as well. Discerning who was telling me what and which sources to trust took a lot of patience and practice. I didn't fully understand the difference myself until someone asked me to help find a missing dog in another state. My first response to this request was, "I'm not sure I can do that… I just talk to dead people." I prayed to St. Francis, tuned in and, much to my amazement, was able to help them track down the dog. It took two days —the feisty little bugger stayed a step or two ahead of me— but towards the end I asked one of the searchers to take a picture of where they were to confirm what I was seeing, and guess who photobombed them? Yep, Houdini the dog!

How do I now know the difference? Two words: interaction and content. My own Guides are always present and help the others to communicate. If I see someone other than my Guides in Spirit and they are clearly interacting with me in order to better illustrate their personality or relay a message, I know that I am using the gift of mediumship and I am tuned to The Medium Channel in order to connect with someone who has left the physical world. These loving spirits will give me names or show me events that you either experienced together, or that have just happened, in order to validate their identity and the fact that they are still with you. They might bring up your health or someone else's as another way of showing their continuing care and concern. General psychic information coming from my Guides, on the other hand, might involve more detailed, preventative health or medical information, or future career and relationship advice which, unless your loved one was psychic in the physical world, they would not be able to diagnose or predict from the afterlife. If this is the case, I am tuned into The Psychic Channel, which is what you will more than likely begin tuning into as you hone your intuition and develop your abilities. Clients often instinctively know what is being relayed by their loved ones versus information that I am getting elsewhere during a reading but, in the event that they don't, I always enjoy interpreting and explaining the difference.

At the very outset of my career, I hesitated to do what I call general psychic or non-mediumship readings. There were two reasons for this. One: as I explained, not all psychics are mediums, so I felt that I was best honoring my gift and serving the greater good by focusing on helping and healing those who were grieving the loss of loved ones. Furthermore, because I am a medium —and let's face it, there aren't that many legit mediums around, I had never run into one in my daily life—, your people (or your friends' people) will find me and pop in during your "general" reading so, in essence, most of my readings end up involving both channels, or the entire Spiritnet. Two: I have found that some people are freaked out by the idea of talking to dead people, and what many of those clients wanted to know about was the future of their relationship or, more specifically, validation that their significant other was a dirt bag or a cheater as they suspected. Trust me (and your own intuition), if you are asking those questions, you don't need to pay me to confirm what you already know. If you truly believe these things are true, it's probably time to take out the trash and kick Don Juan to the curb. It's also important to note that your loved ones can give their opinion on your love life (and mothers and grandmothers just love giving advice from the other side), but they do not know anything beyond what you are privy to about the status of your relationship because they are only connected energetically to *you*, not the other party in question. Shout-out to my patient and loving cousin, Sarah, who helped me to learn this little lesson the hard way! The good news is that general or future information always comes into play during a mediumship reading as well, so if you'd like to book a reading with a psychic medium but you are currently more concerned about your health, career or relationships than about connecting with anyone in spirit, by all means do so, just be prepared for mediumship to be involved and to graciously welcome any unexpected visitors who may pop in with a message for you or someone you know.

5 THE GOOD, THE BAD AND THE UGLY

Who's Who in the Spirit World

By now you've probably noticed me using the terms Spirit World and Other Side when talking about the dimension that exists beyond what we can see, hear and touch in the physical world. If you are Catholic or any other denomination of Christianity, you probably think of this world in terms of the Afterlife or Heaven, Purgatory (aka Limbo) and Hell. I'll touch on the role of religion a bit more when we get to the nuts and bolts of protecting oneself spiritually, but in order to understand who's who in this dimension, you need to first understand a bit of how it's structured.

Whenever people ask me what it's like "up there," the first thing I say is, "The good news is, there is no Hell —at least not as it is depicted in books and movies, with flames and snarling hounds licking at your nether regions for all of eternity. The bad news is, there is no Hell —this can be a bummer to hear if you are counting on the murderers and pedophiles getting their due come Judgment Day." More good news: although they are not cast into a burning pit for all of eternity, there are many, many levels in the afterlife (which is actually more of a "between lives" space where souls prepare for reincarnation), and these jokers are in what I think of as Soul Detention or reform school, which is monitored much more closely than the Saturday School depicted in *The Breakfast Club*. These stubborn and willful souls basically have fewer freedoms. They can't just grab the bathroom pass and head to the loo the way the rest of us, who follow most or all of the school rules can. In any event, rest assured that unless you have been killing people and hoarding body parts in your basement freezer, you won't be running into the likes of Ted Bundy or Jeffrey Dahmer after passing through the Pearly Gates.

Rather than the three-tiered Heaven-Purgatory-Hell afterlife that is accepted by most western religions, the Spirit World is, as I said, comprised of many levels, usually called dimensions, planes or realms. The number of levels is debatable, but most agree that there are several primary planes of existence, each with numerous sub-levels. I have read a lot about these planes of existence but am by no means a scholar on the subject, so I choose to speak or write only about those that I have personally encountered or have been shown knowledge of in my travels between worlds. This means that you'll be hearing a rather simplified explanation of the four main planes of existence as I understand them. I'll also be using lots of analogies involving school because, having spent over two thirds of my life in them as either a student or teacher, that's what I relate to best. Everyone has at some point in their lives done time in the school system (willing or not), so it's a decent common ground that should give you a more solid frame of reference for the extraterrestrial (not of this earth) dimensions that most have had very little, if any, contact with. Some of you may not have had the most positive experiences in school or with the school powers that be, but for the purposes of illustrating who's who on the Other Side, please just assume that this afterlife "school" is a place you would be happy to spend time in and that all of the players described are positive role models in their profession. Pretend it's the Board of Ed from *Boy Meets World*, as opposed to *Breaking Bad*.

The Physical & Astral Planes
Incarnate Souls and Discarnate Souls or "Students"
Starting from the ground (literally) up, you have the Physical Plane, which is where you are currently residing if you are alive. It is also the dwelling ground of "stuck" souls and the discarnate entities that we refer to as "ghosts." I put the term stuck in quotations because no soul is actually stuck here. Any soul that I have encountered here has either been confused (perhaps died suddenly and did not realize they were deceased) or has *chosen* to remain here. Sometimes a soul will choose to be "stuck" here out of fear of judgment on the Other Side. This is often the case with souls who have committed suicide or some other so-called "crime" against the church. If this is the case, it's my job to help deprogram or un-brainwash them so that they can cross over into a more peaceful space without fear. For the record, those who have committed suicide are not punished in any way, shape or form. They are treated with exceptional care as their fractured souls are healed in the loving light beyond. Sometimes a soul will choose to hang around down here because it is their happy place. Many spouses of fifty years or more refuse to leave the sides of their other half and stick around until their husband or wife is ready to join them in the afterlife. My grandparents were married for seventy

years when my grandpa died, and my grandma has seen him and physically felt him with her in bed. His presence is so strong that he blew out two light bulbs and an electrical socket with his energy during one of my visits. In terms of schooling, you might consider the physical or earthly plane grades K-12, because every human being experiences them whether they want to or not. The average lifespan is about 85 years these days and although that may seem like a long time to the younger readers out there, it is the blink of an eye in the grand scheme of things, and souls who choose to incarnate (or hook up with a body and become human) can gain a lot of knowledge in a short amount of time, relatively speaking. If you've ever asked yourself why you are here or what the meaning of life is, the answer is quite simple: To Learn. Your soul *chose* to come here to learn. Your soul also *chose* the family and circumstances into which you were born. This is a nice little nugget of wisdom to throw out, by the way, the next time your snarky or entitled teenager declares that they *"Never asked to be born!"* Ah, but you did, my friend, so suck it up and start learning from your mistakes instead of blaming them on your parents; they've got their own life lessons to master.

While our souls are incarnate (living in a body on Earth), we are meant to learn as much as we possibly can before moving on. The same is true after death, when we shed our corpses and our discarnate souls move on to reside elsewhere in the Universe. Rather than hanging around or being "stuck" here on the Physical Plane, most souls choose to cross over into the Astral Plane. This dimension is also made up of many different levels, several of which you will most likely spend time on depending on how advanced your soul is or what lessons you still need to learn. This is the dimension that is referred to when we talk about the Other Side or crossing over into The Light. I compare this plane or dimension to what Americans refer to as being "in College" (most other countries call it being "at University"), because it is where souls go to continue the learning process and gain higher knowledge upon shedding the human body, or (to continue the analogy), upon graduating from the K-12 Physical Plane. As a medium, I am most familiar with these first two planes because most of the spirits with whom I communicate are either stuck on (or visiting) the Physical Plane or residing on some level of the Astral Plane. Undergrads, Grad students and PhD candidates are all "at University" but not on the same level, so they are taking classes in different buildings and don't run into each other on campus. The same goes for souls on different levels of the Astral Plane. Those who have not yet learned to work and play well with others (the dirty rotten scoundrels of the Afterlife) can still inhabit The Light, but they won't be roaming the same halls as the ever patient and loving kindergarten teacher who is remembered fondly by all. In other words, although Jack the Ripper and my own amazing kindergarten teacher, Mrs. Stewart, would both be welcomed into and embraced by The Light, they won't be mixing and mingling. You would find Jack on a much lower level, chillin' with the villains, while Mrs. Stewart might have moved straight to Guide level, assigned to help another teacher struggling to get through life as an elementary educator on the Physical Plane. Many of your people (deceased friends and family members) on the Other Side may be on the same level, but some may be on different levels, or on the same level but in different "classrooms", based on what they need to focus on. When you schedule a reading with me or any other medium, however, they must all gather on the same level in order to meet the medium halfway. This common ground is usually the lowest common level for two reasons. One, souls in the lower levels do not have access to the elevator key to the higher levels, but those in the higher levels can come and go freely or hop on and press a lower floor button and "go slumming" so to speak if they choose. Two, the lower they convene, the closer they are to the Physical Plane, which means it takes less energy and is therefore easier to communicate with the medium, who is basically an earthling with an extra-long blue tooth antenna. This is also the dimension visited by people who have had an OBE (Out of Body Experience) or NDE (Near Death Experience). If you have ever experienced a visitation from a deceased loved one while in the dream state, you may have unknowingly visited this dimension as well because that is the level where such reunions occur.

People who are on life support, in a coma or in the advanced stages of dementia are also able to communicate from the space between the physical and Spiritual planes. They are not tethered to their physical bodies the same way that most of us are and they pop in during readings (or when I'm going about my daily business) in much the same way that deceased souls do. The first time this happened I assumed that a friend's grandmother had passed away and was reaching out to her through me. I had not spoken to the friend in years, and when I contacted her with Grandma's message, she informed me that she was in the end stages of Alzheimer's. The message had flowed like any other I'd received and everything that she shared made perfect sense, which is how I came to understand that this can happen as well. This message was perhaps more comforting to her family than hearing from her after death because I was able to assure them that she was still herself somewhere in there —and doing just fine— despite what her quality of life might appear to be to those on the outside. Grandma's only complaint was one that could be easily remedied; without her dentures (which she showed me were on the bedside table), she couldn't eat and enjoy the chocolate treats that she had once loved! This lesson brought me great peace as well because I knew that I would be able to communicate with my own mother as her dementia got worse.

The Spiritual Plane:
The Spiritual Leaders or "School Administrators"

Still further up the ladder is the Spiritual Plane. This dimension is populated by very advanced souls. The great thinkers, philosophers and spiritual leaders who seemed to be "on another level" during their time here on Earth reside here. These are the equivalent of the administrators of a school system; the assistant principals, principals or deans of individual schools within a university who convene regularly to discuss and organize the school's curriculum so that no child is left behind. There are no arguments or blow-ups on this level because these souls have mastered their emotions and can think about and discuss the greater good without conflict. There is very little to no ego in this dimension, so you wouldn't find a Donald Trump or Nancy Pelosi in this neck of the woods. These souls are all about the greater good, so you might instead bump shoulders with the likes of Aristotle, Socrates, Abraham Lincoln or the Jimmy and Rosalynn Carters of the political world.

The Celestial or Angelic Plane
Ascended Masters and Angels or "School Board Members"

The highest of the dimensions is the Celestial or Angelic Plane. This is the realm of the Ascended Masters: Jesus, Buddha, Ghandi, St. Anthony, and Martin Luther King Jr., to name but a few. Continuing the school analogy, these are the School Board Members who oversee and govern all that goes on in the lower dimensions and realms. If you pray to the saints as I do, you are calling on one of these loving spirits who are all too happy to assist with everyday miracles, be it healing your heart or finding your car keys. As the name suggests, this dimension also houses the Angels. I especially like the school board analogy here because just as Angels have never been human, many elected School Board Members have never been teachers or administrators, yet they are deemed wise enough to decide what happens in the ranks beneath them in the trenches. These are the souls whom many people automatically pray to when they seek help from Above. Each of us has Guardian Angels assigned to us as well, and you can call on them, as well as any of the Archangels, day or night, should you be in need of divine assistance or intervention. The key is that you *must ask* for their help. They are not allowed to intervene unless directly requested to do so, except in cases of extreme urgency, like if you are about to die in a car crash before your predestined exit point. In those cases, they swoop in and save the day, as depicted in the miraculous true stories you have probably read (and perhaps scoffed at) online. You might ask the Angels for help getting through a difficult time or for extra protection at night so that you get a solid eight hours of sleep when you are especially worn out or have an important interview the next day. This little insight was a game changer for me. Once I realized I could get a good night's sleep, unmolested by the less patient entities out there who love to bug the crap out of mediums in the wee hours, I started beefing up night time security by requesting Angelic reinforcement and haven't looked back since. Please try not to get too carried away with your requests. Don't expect the Angels to help you out at the BINGO parlor or magically do the dishes and laundry whilst you take a happy nappy in the afternoon. It is also important to note that they sometimes respond to a request in unexpected or less direct ways, by sending signs your way that are meant to guide you in the right direction. When I began toying with the idea of writing a book versus a couple of other endeavors I asked for divine guidance, and suddenly everywhere I looked there were advertisements for how to become an author or publish a book. It took me awhile to discern between my Angels and my Guides, but once I figured out their callsigns I was pleasantly surprised to discover that my Angels were as close at hand as my trusted Spirit Guides. I now know that when the left side of my head tingles, it's my Angels telling me to be extra cautious or *think* before I act. If the right side of my head is set abuzz, I know that I will need to be more thoughtful and loving in whatever situation is about to arise. It's kind of like those cartoons where someone has an angel on one shoulder and a devil on the other, only mine are both angels, whispering only good advice in my ears.

I rarely come into contact with beings from the highest realms or levels from this plane of existence (I can only assume they have bigger fish to fry), but when I do, there is no mistaking it. I experience a much richer, deeper tone or frequency in my left ear, or awaken to a powerful presence, outlined in a blinding white light. When They visit, I know there is an important lesson ahead and I bust a move out of bed no matter what the hour may be. In my experience, the highest of these beings usually go by a single word, such as

"Love" or "Compassion" or "Will." Along with the lesson du jour, they also bring with them enough energy to make candle flames go from an inch to eight or ten inches high; they can make a compass needle vibrate as fast as a hummingbird's wings and point due North when in fact it should read South East. I'm not exaggerating in the slightest. I have experienced both of these phenomena and more firsthand. It is thanks to the love and guidance of these Beings of Light that I found the willpower to banish red wine and margaritas from my diet (no small sacrifice for yours truly) before interacting with or opening myself up to the Other Side. Now, I will not touch alcohol within twelve hours of a reading aimed at connecting you with your lost loved ones because of a little chat that I had with one such miracle worker from the Spirit World.

The Highest Plane
God/Source or "The Superintendent"
At the helm of the Celestial Plane (and of all creation), resides the head of the school system, aka the Superintendent, aka God, the Divine Creator, The Great Spirit, The One, Source or whatever you choose to call the Highest Power in the Universe. No matter what name you prefer, they represent the divine, loving creative force made up of pure love and light which is responsible for all that is good on both sides of the veil. Contrary to popular belief, Spirit has shown me (and a gazillion other humans across the millennia) that this divine being does not care what you call Them, nor what religion or faith you subscribe to, so long as you are doing your best to follow the Golden Rule and treat others the way you wish to be treated. All energy originates and flows from this creative source and, like any good Superintendent, they just want every pupil —which in this case, is every soul— to do their best to

learn and grow during their time in "school" here on Earth and between lives.

Across the Universe
Spirit Guides or "The Teachers"

This bit may seem out of order, but these spiritual beings can reside on any number of the planes described above, depending on who it is they are assigned to guide. Now that you have a general idea of the structure and hierarchy of the Spirit World, it's time to talk about the souls who I believe deserve the most attention (and praise) from each of us — drumroll please— our Spirit Guides. We all have Human Guides that we encounter here on Earth. These are the people whom the Universe puts in our path to help us grow and learn in some way. Grandparents, parents and teachers are probably the first people who come to mind, but they can be friends, spouses or anyone else who comes into your life and helps you to grow and understand yourself better. I have personally been guided by many friends, family members and wonderful educators, who not only taught me the basics, but made me love school so much that I was inspired to become a teacher myself. We each also have several of these amazing "teachers" supporting us from the Other Side throughout our journey on the physical plane. Our Primary or Main Guide is with us from birth until death, while others come and go as needed at different points in our lives, just like the Earthly Guides who come in and out of our lives. For about ten years before I became one myself, I consulted another trusted psychic medium about once a year. At some point during each session the psychic, Bob, would refer to one of his two trusty Spirit Guides, Fletcher and Rose. Though I was a somewhat regular customer and obviously not a skeptic, I'll admit that I could never really wrap my head around the whole Spirit Guide thing. To be honest, they seemed a bit silly, like imaginary friends to me... until I started hearing from the Spirit World myself and realized how important they are not just to psychics, but to every living soul. One of the homework assignments I'm going to give you later in this book is to begin trying to get in touch with your Guides. This is sometimes trickier than you would think, and there are two schools of thought here. Some psychics claim to be able to tell you they know who your Guides are (in my experience they will more often than not tell you said Guides are of Native American descent), but others feel that you alone can make contact with and identify your Spirit Guides. I subscribe to the second school and I'll tell you why. First, although I am always aware of the fact that every reading I do involves the assistance and cooperation of my Guides and the Guides of anyone else present, of the *hundreds* of readings I've done involving *thousands* of friendly and not-so-friendly Spirits, I have never once encountered one who identified themselves as someone's Spirit Guide. Second, the only time I have encountered a Native American is if someone happened to be of that heritage. In other words, I have not personally experienced a mini tribe of Native Americans on the Other Side, smoking peace pipes and claiming Guide credit. Does this mean that it is not possible? Absolutely not. There is a wide range of varied gifts among mediums. I'm simply telling you to be wary of anyone who straight up names any of your Guides, especially if they charge you extra to do it. At the very least, you should trust your own instincts about what you are being told.

That is exactly what I tell clients who want to get in touch with their Spirit Guides. Look within and trust your instincts.

Here is how it has played out when I have been asked to help someone with the task of meeting and greeting their Guides, and why I believe you must ultimately be the one to identify and name your own Guides. The developing psychics and mediums who come to me for tutoring are often frustrated, wondering about a presence that they sense or a name that they keep hearing. Who or what might it be? Is it their Spirit Guide? Is it a ghost? Are they just going crazy? I completely understand their frustration, as you will see when I share what I went through getting to know my own Guides, but the best I can do is to help them to clarify what they are hearing, seeing or feeling as they discern what or whom they are dealing with. The first of my psychic students who brought up the question of Spirit Guides came in hoping that I could help her to understand all of the strange things she had been experiencing. Based on what she shared, it was pretty clear to me that she had a lot of psychic potential. When I asked if she was in law enforcement or something that involved investigations, she said she had graduated the day before with a degree in Criminal Justice and hoped to be a detective. I then asked her if she knew a Tom, and that's when our discussion about Spirit Guides began. She had been hearing the name *Thomas* over and over, at home upon waking, in the car while driving past a cemetery, and anywhere else you can imagine. She hadn't *seen* anything as of yet, but she had been sensing a presence and experiencing other things that could not be passed off as mere coincidence, such as feeling compelled one day to look inside of a military hat that she had found in a closet at school, only to find the name "THOMAS" written in Sharpie on the inner rim. My own Guides told me to try an exercise that I had used in the past when others had come to me looking to validate a presence that they had seen or felt. I tuned in to see what or whom I might pick up on, and it turned out to be a somewhat creepy silver-haired older man, with a drunk's bristly stubble, a paunchy stomach and anything *but* the best of intentions. This concerned me a bit to say the least, but I scribbled down my impressions and forged ahead, asking her if she could conjure up a physical description of the presence she had been feeling, despite the fact that she hadn't seen anything. Almost instantly she was able to say that she felt it was a younger male with dark hair who shared some specific emotional traits with her, and whom she felt was very protective of her. She was somewhat confused when I seemed excited that I had not been picked up on the same traits and had been unable to validate her impressions of Thomas, but that was precisely how I knew that he had to be a highly *personal* protective energy (e.g. a Guide). If it had been anything else, a deceased relative, friend or some other random spirit who had chosen to attach himself to her, I would have seen and come up with the same or a very similar description, as happens during most readings and paranormal investigations that I conduct. This method has worked every time since, and it is now my go-to way of helping others dig deep, examine their gut feelings, trust their own instincts and identify who's by their side guiding, as opposed to haunting, them. This is one of the many examples of how my Guides continue to teach *me* when I am teaching others. P.S. I ran into the creepy old dude again the next day during a paranormal investigation. He turned out to be a crusty pervert hanging around the home of two attractive females and my description of him fit their impressions to a T. The one telltale sign of a Guide that you must be aware of is this: even if you are a wee bit freaked out by sensing an otherworldly presence, a Guide will *always* feel loving and protective, as opposed to sketchy or scary. If the presence does not feel like they are a personal cheerleader, in your corner, or bringing you some measure of comfort or joy, you may be dealing with what I call *The Crust*.

Remember when I alluded to the fact that I am sometimes a slow learner? Recognizing my Guides was one such occasion. I had been receiving and delivering messages from Spirit regularly for at least six months before I was able to separate my hard-working, ever-present Guides from the deceased friends and family members who popped in to visit. I had seen someone on the Other Side who felt very familiar and reminded me a lot of myself, and had heard the name Amanda at the beginning of so many messages that it got to be a running joke as I asked one person after another, "Do you have an Amanda? Puh-lease tell me you have an Amanda?" There were never any takers, which was unusual because Spirit is pretty darn good when it comes to names; I don't always get them, but when I do, nine times out of ten they "fit" and we move on. Finally, after an especially spot-on and music-filled message, I was (yet again) wondering to myself who this Amanda was when I heard the theme song to a Nickelodeon show from the 90's, "Aman-Aman-Aman-Aman-Aman-da Show" and suddenly it clicked: Amanda was my Main Guide, helping me "run the show" as I received and delivered messages as a medium. She sometimes appears as a conductor or a deejay before readings, or as an air traffic controller when there's a lot of "traffic" from the Spirit World heading my way or I need to help a soul crossover into The Light. Her presence is always a comfort and I am always happy to see or hear from her, though this happens less frequently now that we have worked out our own unique call signs. All it takes is a specific little pulse and she has my full attention. Your Main Guide is with you from birth until death and, rather than being someone who was directly related to you, is a soul who had a lot in common with you during their stay on the Physical Plane. A great-grandmother who died before you were born or a beloved grandmother who recently passed can certainly act as a Family Guide, watching over you and looking out for your welfare, but your Main Guide is most likely someone who had a similar upbringing or the same profession, for instance. Most importantly, they faced many of the same challenges and had the same overriding life lessons to learn, which is what makes them so well-suited to the job of helping you get through grades K-12 on the Physical Plane. In addition to sharing life lessons with me, Amanda and my other Spirit Guides were either mothers, teachers, or psychic mediums at some point during their time here on earth. Another perk of getting to know your Guides is that it is impossible to feel lonely once you are aware of their presence. I've always been an unabashed and confessed self-talker, but now when I'm caught chattering away to no one, I can declare with all honesty that I'm just chewing the fat with Amanda, Mickey or whichever other Guide I might need advice from at the moment. I'm sure that sounds as kooky to you as it did to me when Bob would go off on a Guide tangent with Fletcher and Rose. All I can say to that is the Spirit Guide phenomenon is proof that truth is often stranger than fiction! For me, my own Guides are true rock stars of the Spirit World, having guided me so quickly (and safely) from confused amateur ghost whisperer to confident professional medium.

Speaking of safety, I would be remiss in not drawing special attention to the Spirit Guides known as Gatekeepers, who play a critical role in terms of protection, especially to those of us who interact with the Spirit World daily. Gatekeepers are the bouncers at the door of your aura or personal spiritual space, making sure that no one slips into the club looking for trouble or having not paid the cover fee. They keep what you might call the spiritual riff raff (aka The Crust) from mucking around with or clogging up the Spirit Channels so that you can receive clearly. As I shared earlier, some Spirit Guides are with you from birth, some come later and stick around, and some help in a certain capacity and then move on. Such was the case with my Gatekeepers. I'm not for certain who had the job of guarding my personal spiritual space to begin with, but it could not have been easy because the first one didn't last long, and I was constantly being reminded by Amanda to put up the velvet barriers in order to bar the pesky hangers on who wanted to get into *Club Beth* sans invite once I rolled out the red carpet to the Spirit World.

About a year or so into my journey on the road to professional mediumship, I met an exceptional father on the Other Side who reminded me of Magnum P.I. (the *original* Magnum, Tom Selleck, not the new knock-off). He was not only handsome and charming, but also the father-in-law of a friend, so I was all too happy to assist with his messages from the Spirit World. After spending a lot of time with him as the carrier pigeon of said messages, I began to truly appreciate what an exceptional communicator he was —Shout Out to the Geminis here and in Spirit— they are always amazing! He also had incredible stamina. In the span of an hour this man could use the electrical circuits and radio to pull every trick in the Spirit Playbook in order to validate his presence. One day, after a particularly fun-filled morning with him, I wondered aloud why *he* couldn't be one of my Guides. I no sooner had asked that before my head started to tingle and I saw him standing next to Amanda and another of my Guides. They shook hands and Amanda pinned that universally recognized star-shaped brass broach to his uniform, which I understood to mean that there was a new Sheriff in town, protecting the gate. The Sheriff did (and still does) an amazing job, but in the end — due to my spazzy energy attracting far too many wayward Spirits like drunken moths to a brightly lit saloon— someone Up There decided I needed at least two Gatekeepers. The fact that I am often called upon to help many of these unsettled Spirits crossover was also a factor in needing added security at the gate. About that time, as I was chatting with someone's grandmother in the Spirit World, I noticed my dad being shown around by one of my Guides. He had passed away the year before and I hadn't seen him for a while, so I assumed that he had finally settled into his new routine on the Other Side and had dropped by for the nickel tour. I knew he would think it was cool because he had experienced it firsthand just before he died. Sometime later, however, while coaxing a rather unruly Spirit into The Light with the help of Amanda and The Sheriff, I caught a glimpse of my dad sitting on the bench of a playing field. He seemed to be patiently waiting to be called into the game. The moment that I realized what was happening was, as you can imagine, one of the happiest I had experienced since becoming a medium, and this match made perfect sense. My dad's favorite song was Jim Croce's, "You Don't Mess Around with Jim," and for good reason. At 6'2", 230 lbs., and with hands made strong by years in the construction field, Jim Parker had always been a guy that you didn't want to mess with. He was all bark, no bite when it came to my brother and me, but we'd heard the tales of (and witnessed the hands broken from) the brawls he engaged in from his mid-teens through his mid-forties, mostly in the ice hockey rink or at the bar. He may have been a tad overprotective of his only daughter as well, not unlike Liam Neeson's character in the *Taken* movies. Now that he's a member of my personal Spirit World A-Team, I know that I'm in good hands, especially when he rolls up to the scene in his Gator golf cart sporting brass knuckles. Unsurprisingly, I ceased being followed into the shower by a certain unwelcome ghost just after my dad succumbed to lung cancer and joined him on the Other Side. There have been a few times when The Sheriff has had to step in and hold Dad back when it became clear that he was getting a bit overzealous in his handling of some lecherous discarnate thug that he didn't want coming too close to me. The reason I've spent so much time on the role of this uber important Guide, aside from getting to boast about my own superhero Gatekeepers, is to emphasize how important security is when you are dealing with the good, the bad and the ugly of the Spirit World.

PART II:
SPIRITUAL PROTECTION AND ENERGY BALANCING

A PSYCHIC'S GUIDE TO STAYING SANE

I recently watched a fascinating documentary called *Heal* on Netflix, it is about the mind's miraculous ability to heal the body, or how belief can shift biology. The remainder of the documentary showcases what is being done outside the field of traditional western medicine to help people heal. Thank you, Netflix, for teaching us about something that, in my own humble opinion, is far more constructive and life affirming than how to create a meth lab in the Science wing of the local high school. I highly recommend that you watch it in its entirety, but I was particularly struck by a couple of salient points that were made, and I immediately knew that I *must* include them in some way here. Parapsychology is defined as the study of mental phenomena which are excluded from or inexplicable by orthodox scientific psychology. Those in this field, especially psychics and mediums, often refer to an intangible force or entity called *Spirit*. I spend most of my waking (and some of my slumbering) hours interacting with this unique force and I have been blathering on and on about Spirit-this and Spirit World-that ad nauseum in this book. Watching this documentary, however, gave me a fresh perspective on the energy or energies that fall under this rather generalized term. We currently use the word Spirit to describe a supernatural being or ghost, or the non-physical part of a person which houses our emotions and character (aka the soul). We also frequently use it to describe the way a person or group behaves (e.g. "Boy, those fans sure have a lot of spirit!"). According to this film, however, way back in the day spirit was defined as, "invisible moving forces that influence the physical realm," and I can't reason with why that does not pop up as the first definition when you google the word, because it is a far more apt description of an otherwise vague term we throw around so freely in the psychic world. Whether we are talking about Spirit, Spirits (plural) or anything in the Spirit World, in each case we are referring to energies or forces which can rarely if ever be seen —at least not by the "normal" naked eye— but the effects of which can often be seen or felt and, more importantly, which can have a great impact on our own personal energy fields.

What does all of this have to do with you raising your own vibration and opening up to the Universe in the hopes of sharpening your own intuitive or psychic instincts? Every single thing in the Universe, tangible and intangible, is made up of energy, and the more open you are to those parts of the Universe that can't be seen (those energies that reside in your new playground, the Spiritnet), the more these energies, be they fun and friendly new playmates or playground bullies, can affect you. A good majority of those reading this are empaths, which is a fancy word for someone who is highly sensitive to energy. If you are an empath, as a child you walked onto the playground and instantly sensed and soaked in everything around you, which is why they are sometimes referred to as "energy sponges." Simply put, empaths are clairsentients on steroids. Psychic or not, all empaths are subject to the perils of feeling what others feel and they must learn to separate their own energy and emotions from the energy and emotions of, say, the sad girl sitting all alone in the lunchroom, or the borderline narcissist who trolls the room like a human slow cooker full of simmering rage, looking for the weakest kid so he can steal their lunch. The empath might cry just looking at the girl eating alone or feel inexplicably ramped up or on edge in the presence of the bully. Far too many empaths go through life completely unaware of the fact that the up and down feelings they experience throughout the day may be based on the people they are around as opposed to being generated from within their own internal ecosystem. They go from doctor to psychologist to psychiatrist, trying to find some chemical or biological explanation for their anxieties and ever-changing emotions. I am *not* a doctor (nor a martyr) and I am a firm believer in using whatever modern medicine has to offer to ease your suffering, be it psychological or physical; I am simply suggesting that there are other ways to manage some, if not all of these symptoms, through energy balancing and meditation. Wherever you fall on the Empath Scale, you will benefit greatly from the information and activities presented in this section of the book. If you are currently exercising your psychic superpowers on a regular basis, or if you plan to in the future, what I am about to share with you could literally save your sanity. I would love to give credit to each and every source that has helped me come up with these tips and tricks because they more than kept me sane as I ventured quite cluelessly into the great unknown, but that would be impossible. Please just know that everything presented here is an amalgamation of all that I have learned, and that I am deeply indebted, once again, not only to my Spirit Guides, but also to the many others who came before me who were generous enough to share their knowledge.

If you've made it this far without getting impatient and going straight to the hands-on part of the book, please do not skip ahead now because what you are about to read is perhaps the most important lesson that I have to share; how to protect yourself from the unsavory entities that can be found in the Spirit World. When I drew up the lesson plans for my first psychic development circle, I put this one first because, before you try to break the vibration barrier and get in touch with your Spirit Guides, it is imperative that you learn to protect yourself psychically and spiritually in some manner. I will share what I do and try to keep it as non-denominational as possible, but the bottom line is that just as one needs to protect themselves from the hazards of the Physical Plane, be they internet trolls, robocallers or STDs, so must one protect themselves from the negative energies who can just as easily catfish you when you venture online into the vast Spiritnet.

You've probably seen scary movies involving demonic possession, and maybe even messed around with seances or a Ouija Board at slumber parties, but in reality what you are most likely to encounter are the insidious little time-wasters I touched on a bit earlier; those that I lovingly refer to as The Crust of the Spirit World. I've read and seen *The Exorcist,* and

I'm not saying that demons and other supremely shady entities don't exist, but I have yet to come into contact with anything of the sort (unless you count the roommate I had freshman year of college, whom I am still convinced was possessed by *something*). The point is, I can neither confirm nor deny their existence because I *always always always* make it a point to protect myself morning and night, especially before venturing into large crowds or doing any paranormal investigations. I highly recommend that the protection rituals I share, or others of your own choosing, become as much a part of your daily routine as brushing and flossing your teeth. Before we delve into how to protect yourself psychically, however; I must digress a bit and touch on the touchy subject of religion and the power of prayer.

6 INTANGIBLE PROTECTION

The Power of Prayer

You may have noticed that when I was describing the different planes of existence, I mentioned Jesus and Buddha as co-habitants of the highest Celestial Plane. This was no mistake. You may have been told that only "Good Christians" go to Heaven, with all other unbaptised souls being banished to purgatory (if they are lucky) or Hell (if they are not). That is, quite frankly, just a load of bull used to scare people into following a set of rules deemed appropriate by I'm not sure who, but it wasn't Jesus. He, and the rest of the crew who have made it to that highest realm, which is closest to the Source of all creation, love every soul equally, regardless of their race, gender or creed. To be clear, I am neither agnostic, atheist, nor anti-religion. Despite the fact that I was raised without the influence of any organized religion (and still do not practice in any formal fashion), I have complete faith in God and the Universe, and I pray daily. My mother was raised in the Catholic faith and I was christened in the Church, but she had apparently been scarred for life by what she called the "scary nuns and priests and creepy chanting in Latin," so my only childhood experience with church or liturgy was at the weddings of relatives from her large Italian family. My father was raised by a Baptist mother and Methodist father but had shied away from organized religion as well. His only parochial advice to us growing up was to "Live by the Golden Rule." I looked this rule up as a kid and decided that he was correct, and that if everyone would abide by it all of humanity would coexist peacefully, and I left it at that. Around the age of twelve I asked my mother if we could go to church so that I could see what all the fuss was about. After an hour or two of Sunday School, which was held in a dank basement and turned out to be nothing more than a dozen tweens around a long table, taking turns reading scripture —poorly, I might add, for only a few of them could pronounce the word disciple correctly— I decided to pack it in and go it alone with God as I had been. My older brother shared this overall first impression. He only made it about halfway through the class before excusing himself to go to the bathroom. From there he and his friend made like Elvis and left the building entirely, ghosting the rest of us less gutsy rule-followers. My favorite comedian, Ricky Gervais, is an Atheist, but his NetFlix series *Derek* is full of the same "Golden Rule" truths espoused by most churches, minus the religious rhetoric. I re-watch this show whenever I need to restore my faith in humanity or put my personal problems in perspective. My favorite quote from the lovable autistic title character is, "I've met people who believe in God that are good and that are bad. And I've met people who don't believe in God that are good and that are bad. So, just be good." I feel this is sage advice, regardless of what you do or don't believe.

I was (and am) definitely a "believer" and have always had an open mind about all religions. I found that I was equally fascinated by the stories of the saints that I learned from my mothers-in-law (all of whom were Catholic) as I was by the books I read about reincarnation and past lives. I lean on St. Francis when I need assistance with something involving animals, St. Jude for children, and Dymphna for mental stability. I've been exceptionally devoted to St. Anthony since my early twenties, having been rescued by him time and time again anytime that I've misplaced or lost something. Whether it be my keys at home or the luggage of twenty students during a school trip abroad, good old Tony has never let me down. As a child, the thing that terrified me the most was anything involving demons and possession, so I also like the idea of being safeguarded by a religion that trains up expert exorcists!

Aside from my almost daily reliance on St. Anthony, when I began hearing from the Spirit World, I was relatively clueless about the true power of prayer and of the necessity of creating some kind of ritual for protecting myself in my new supernatural environment. As luck (or fate) would have it, upon hearing about my newfound ability and my enthusiasm about developing it, a good friend of mine asked me how I was protecting myself from "everything out there." She must have found my response wanting because, God bless her, she sent me John Edward's book, *Infinite Quest*, which was life-changing for me. Here was someone —a famous psychic medium whom I had seen on TV— writing as if he were reading my mind. As I read that book, my head lit up with near-constant tingles after each passage. I could relate to everything he shared; it was as if St. Anthony himself was throwing me signals via psychic stun gun. My morning meditation was hijacked as well. For about two weeks, the pages of my journal were filled with names from the Bible as my Guides worked furiously to fill in the gaps of my rather secular upbringing. David, Solomon, Bathsheba; I had to pause in the dictation of all they were sharing with me every so often to look them up, putting dates and events with the names they were dropping to make sense of it all. Luckily my husband had been raised by a mother who had spent most of her career teaching elementary students in Catholic schools, so I had a couple of well-versed tutors at my disposal. They kept me, or I should say the house, protected with an unending supply of holy water as well.

It may seem as if I'm trying to draw in converts to Catholicism, but that is not the case at all. I still have an open mind about and interest in all religious belief systems, so long as they don't involve shaving my head, selling roses or drinking Kool Aid in Jonestown. I have done readings for and learned much from Muslims, Jews, Hindus and just about every branch of Christianity you can name, and I highly doubt that I would have been given this gift had I not always had a healthy respect for the beliefs of others. I don't feel that you have to subscribe to any one religion at all. I'm going to pay homage to John Edward once again by sharing one of the most profound bits of wisdom I have encountered on the subject of religion. At some point in his career he was doing a show and an audience member asked him, being that he was up close and personal with the Spirit World, which was the "best" religion. I'm paraphrasing here, but his reply was something to the effect of, "What's the best language that is spoken on here on Earth? English, Spanish or Mandarin, because they are the most used? Language is the way man communicates with each other.

Religion is the way man communicates with God." This message still resonates so deeply with me, perhaps because I spent most of my life as a language teacher, that I broke out in goosebumps while typing it again here. I share it as often as I can —and am always sure to give Mr. Edward and his Guides credit— because it so simply and beautifully illustrates a Universal truth that I wish every person on the planet would understand and embrace; that we are all connected on an energetic level to One Source, regardless of what language we speak or which religion we practice.

I am fluent in English and French, conversational in Spanish and Italian, and I use the language of Catholicism to communicate with God, because that is works or "feels right" for me. Bottom line? You can pray to whomever you like — Santa Claus or the Tooth Fairy if that's what floats your boat—– or you may feel perfectly satisfied with some of the other non-denominational, New Age-y protection tools that I'm about to share with you. As I said, I don't formally attend church, but I have personally never felt more connected to the God and the entire Universe thanks to the power of my daily prayer and meditation practices. This is why I feel compelled to share everything that works for me with you. That being said, in case you *are* interested (or are looking to try something new), here is the routine that I use when protecting myself: I start each morning praying the Rosary (an abridged version of it because I'm way too ADD to get through that many Hail Marys), followed by a prayer to St. Anthony (this is when I generally set my intention for the day), St. Patrick's Breastplate Prayer, and a prayer to Archangel Michael (both of which I consider spiritual shields). I close with a prayer to the Angels and another aimed directly at the Holy Spirit. That may sound like a lot, but it takes ten minutes or less and it is time well spent because my Guides usually use it to clue me in as to whom or what I can expect in the day ahead. I also never leave home without my St. Anthony bracelet on my wrist and an Archangel Michael medal tucked in my bra, which may sound absurd to some, but I would personally rather be safe than sorry.

We all know (or may have been) that student who abhors authority and would do absolutely anything to avoid sitting through fifty minutes of English or History class. They will endure even more when it comes to avoiding facing the consequences of their actions. These are the fools who pulled your pigtails in elementary school and threw spitballs across the table in middle school. Anything to get a little attention, be it negative or positive. They were the chronic class cutters in high school who tried to talk you into playing hooky and getting drunk or stoned with them, and who made Ferris Bueller look like an amateur. These same souls can be found roaming the hallways between worlds, with nothing better to do than waste your time. And waste it they will, or worse, if you do not learn how to block them from your Spirit Friend List. Prayer in any form is, in my opinion, the ultimate weapon of warfare against these uninvited visitors, but I can appreciate that some of you are neither familiar nor comfortable with anything that smacks of religion, so I've sprinkled in a few non-denominational or Universal tools. What matters most is not which you choose to use, but the intention that you bring while using them.

HOMEWORK ASSIGNMENT #1

Protecting Yourself Spiritually

If you do nothing else in terms of protecting yourself before opening yourself to the Spirit World, please memorize the following (or write it on a notecard and keep it handy):

"I encircle myself in the white light of God's love and divine protection. I am only open to communicating with those souls who walk in this white light, and who are dedicated to serving the greater good."

As you say these words (either silently or aloud), imagine a golden white light pouring down from the clouds —you know the kind that breaks through, making it look like there is a crack in Heaven— and encasing your entire body like an oversized halo or magical cocoon. If you get hung up on the word God, substitute the words "The Universe" or whatever word(s) feel right to you.

Whichever version you decide upon, learn it and say it anytime you plan on connecting to the Universe via the Spiritnet. *Period.* This is a simple yet highly effective shield against anything sinister found in the Dark Web of the Spiritnet. Think of the cocoon of golden white light as a psychic condom or anti-virus software. Because I am a medium, and therefore basically a beacon sending out a more or less constant signal to the Spirit World, I say this each morning before I begin the prayer ritual that I described above. I also repeat it anytime I walk into a location that gives me the heebie jeebies, like a haunted house or my local Walmart.

7 TANGIBLE PROTECTION

Holy Water, Sage and Talismans, Oh My!

In addition to prayer, there are other more tangible methods of spiritually protecting oneself and one's environment. My top picks in this category are holy water, sage, incense, crystals and talismans. I'll cover the first three in greater detail in a moment, and crystals will be getting more than their fair share of attention in chapter 14. As far as talismans go, my St. Anthony bracelet and Archangel Michael medal fall under this last category, as do evil eye trinkets, Hamsa amulets, and anything else designed to ward off evil spirits or keep your personal space free from negative energy. Just like religion, there is no best talisman or protection device. The most important thing in choosing and using one is that it speaks to you personally and that you trust and believe in its ability to keep The Crust at bay.

Now a word on holy water, which is nothing more than tap

water that has been sanctified by a priest for the purpose of blessing people, places, and objects, or as a means of warding off evil. You don't have to take out a loan and travel to some famous religious shrine in Lourdes, France or any other far flung site of religious miracles; you can easily get the generic brand free of charge at your local Catholic church or shrine. Bring a mason jar or thermos from home to collect it in though, because they usually charge for any plastic bottle or container that they provide. We always have a hefty supply on hand in large glass containers which, as I said earlier, my thoughtful mother-in-law keeps replenished. None of the truly wild stuff that I associate with my initiation into mediumship began happening until after I met my husband. I'm certain that the Universe arranged it this way because, rather than be frightened off by an eHarmony profile that read, *Beth, 45, Psychic Medium*, the Powers That Be made sure he was emotionally committed by the time I correctly identified his house ghost by name. As we were each learning to wrap our heads around my new circumstances, and as other mysterious and crazy things began happening chez Wieczynski, he took it all in stride and left the "haints and goblins" to me, with one caveat; that I promise to always keep the holy water fonts topped off. I had no qualms about fulfilling his request and rarely need reminding because if our dog positively refuses to go upstairs, it always turns out that the holy water well hanging at the foot of the steps is bone dry. It also didn't hurt that Scott's beloved Granny Marie was one of the first loving Spirits to pay me a visit and has since become one of my frequent flyers from the Spirit World.

Sage is another staple which should be kept in any psychic's pantry at all times. It usually comes in mini bundles that look like twigs (or joints) tied together in the shape of a yule log or chicken drumstick. Like most wines, it comes in many varieties; California White, for example. Some species smell more like marijuana than Jimmy Dean's finest breakfast meat, which might transport some of you back to the good old days of wake 'n bake. Whatever the scent, sage is used in smudging rituals, which are meant to cleanse a space of any negative or "crusty" energy. I have a basic smudging kit which includes a bundle of sage, a large abalone shell (which basically functions as an ashtray), and a feather to help waft the smoke about. I take this along when called upon to assess the energy of and/or cleanse a home. Frankincense and myrrh incense or Palo Santo sticks are also well-recognized in the field of smudging and are equally effective crust busters. I use the incense at home because my husband has an over developed olfactory system ––his super sniffer rivals that of our dog— and he complains that sage makes our house smell like a sausage factory. I prefer incense sticks to cones because you can simply light them and wave them around like a sparkler or a magic wand, banishing the crusty vibes from your kingdom. As far as I know there is no hard and fast rule about how often one should smudge one's castle. I light incense every day during my morning meditation, but I only smudge the entire house every month or so, unless the air starts feeling heavy or yucky sooner. It's best to keep a window or two open when smudging to let out the bad juju. Take note of how much smoke is produced by the sage or incense; the more there is, the more you needed to de-crustify your space!

8 SPIRITS AND SPIRITS DON'T MIX

An Important Psychic P.S.A.

Protecting your exterior environment is important, but you can also help protect yourself from The Crust by monitoring what goes inside of you. I love my red wine and pizza rolls, and I am the last person you'll find judging what others choose to put into their bodies, but I have learned the hard way that spirits (booze) and spirits (dead peeps) don't mix. I'm not always one hundred percent correct in interpreting messages from the Spirit World when I am stone cold sober, but I have found that I am pretty much always straight up wrong with even simple yes/no, either/or predictions after a glass or two of vino. Because of this I have learned to never, I repeat *never*, operate my psychic powers under the influence of alcohol or any other mind-altering drug. I consider the advice that follows an important PSA for anyone, psychic or not, who is highly sensitive to other energies or wondering why they always seem to come away with more than just your average hangover after overindulging.

I may be the only person who came of age in the 80's that *didn't* try cocaine, including my parents (a fun fact that I learned courtesy of my mother's early onset dementia, which stole her memory and any filter she ever possessed). It wasn't that I was uber wise as a teen or even in my twenties, but I instinctively felt that, given my natural level of spazzy energy, my head might literally pop off if I tried it. Over the years people have mistakenly assumed that I was on coke anyway because of said spazzy energy, so I took Nancy Reagan's advice and *Just Said No*. I did try other things, like pot and 'shrooms, neither of which would I classify as a positive experience. The one and only time I tried an edible, I left half of it on a low table —as I lay physically and mentally wrecked on the couch— and nearly killed my dog who decided to snack on it. My last and (I promise!) final foray into the research of drugs as metaphysical experience enhancers was some South American snuff, whose actual name escapes me, or I would put it here **in bold** as a warning. Suffice it to say that I wound up on the host's bathroom floor throwing up next to a perfectly lovely man who claimed to have been kidnapped by the Illuminati or some such. There are people who feel that certain drugs, especially those that fall under the umbrella of psychedelics, raise their vibration or bring on mystical experiences. I won't argue with them (to each his own), but I have found the exact opposite to be true.

As someone who spends most of their time dealing with all sorts of energies, I can tell you that both drugs *and* alcohol almost always attract the wrong kind of energy from both sides of the veil. I'm a huge fan of the show Drunk History, but when my husband polishes off a twelve pack and launches into his own version of the show, he starts out with a lesson on

Confucius and before you know it he's gone down a Bud Light-fueled rabbit hole and any reference to the ancient philosopher goes out the window, replaced by "General Motherf*ckin' Tso." I have the Snapchat video to prove this and —though I do still find it highly entertaining— I pull it out whenever I am tempted to drink to the point of intoxication.

I'm not saying that you have to give up your glass of wine with dinner, or bottle of beer after a long day, but any time you get completely plastered, you run the risk of lowering your vibration and inviting The Crust into your energy field. Simply put, drugs and alcohol leave you open to psychic attack from bottom dwellers in the Spirit World who get their rocks off by influencing and/or living vicariously through your drunk or stoned self. As a teacher I am all too familiar with energy vampires that exist on on the physical plane; those students and colleagues who bring nothing to the table except a potential headache and insist on finding your last nerve and perching themselves mercilessly upon it. These same creatures exist on the other side and it is important to recognize and avoid them. Refraining from imbibing in anything to excess is one simple way to do dodge these energetic bullets. I'm guessing that you wouldn't willingly hang out with the local crackheads in the "real" world, so why open yourself up to the ones you can't see? As one who *has* seen them, I promise they are not the kind of people you would bring home to meet mom. Feel free to drink up or light up or sniff your way to whatever enlightenment you might find on your gnarly trip across the Universe in search of nirvana, but don't come crying to me when Lucy in the Sky with Diamonds turns out to be a fat bald pedophile catfishing you from the dark side of the moon. If you are reading this and actively trying to develop your own psychic abilities, you're welcome! Trust me, one day you will be thanking me... and so might your dog.

If you ever get to the point where you are offering group readings, you would also be wise to ban alcohol during the event and advise the participants to keep it to a minimum if they are gathering before your arrival. Although I sometimes refer to group readings as "Spirit Parties" and they are meant to be fun, one cocktail might calm any pre-game jitters, but anything more can impair a person's ability to pick up on or fully appreciate the messages that Spirit is sending their way.

9 AURAS 101

Understanding External Energy Fields

Auras are like a full body halo of energy that is generated by and surrounds a person, thing, or place. Your aura is the energy field that emanates from your physical being, or the "vibes" you put off. All of the protection tips shared above are meant to protect this personal energy field. Auras are layered and made up of many colors. Each of these color components of light has its own wavelength and very specific qualities of energy which can affect our emotions. This is why, even if you aren't capable of *seeing* the color or colors in someone's aura, you are probably able to *feel* the vibes those colors sending out into the universe. Some people are able to see auras without trying and know just by the color(s) that they see surrounding someone whether they should smile and say hello, or run, not walk, as far away as possible. I read about one such gifted aura-voyant who could tell if someone was sexually attracted to them, a skill that was surely useful in high school when the rest of the world was worried about asking someone out on a date and potentially being shot down. I have always been able to feel someone's aura or pick up on their vibes. I do not, however, always see the colors surrounding a person when I'm out and about or even during a reading, so when I do, I know that it is more important than usual. It will either be useful to the person seeking my advice on some matter, or for my own personal protection. If someone sits down and I see purple around them, I know that I am in the presence of someone with who is more psychic or intuitive than average, whether they know it yet or not. A green aura lets me know that someone has healing gifts or, if they have faced a recent major illness, that they are in the healing process. It is also important to note that the colored layers of our aura are not set in stone, but in a state of flux depending upon our general health and frame of mind. If I see gray, I know that someone is depressed or not feeling their best, or that they need to get rid of some form of spiritual static that is fogging up their energy field and interfering with their lives in some way. That same person could come back a week later after some daily grounding and energy dumping techniques and the gray will be gone, replaced by a bright white, clean field of light.

There are, of course, many books and websites devoted to this topic, so I won't spend too much time instructing you on the art of aura reading here. The easiest way for me to describe it is that it is similar to what we psychics call "tuning in". Try to more or less focus on a person or object and then slightly un-focus your eyes. If you've ever purposely blurred your vision to appreciate the lights on a Christmas tree from another perspective, you know what I'm talking about. If you haven't, google "aura reading" and try one of the many online training activities out there. Don't get your panties in a bunch if you read a book or go online and try some of the exercises designed to sharpen your aura reading skills to no avail. As I said, most people (myself included) are able to read someone's aura without the technicolor visual ancillary. You probably do it all the time without realizing it. Like when you walk past a stranger or meet someone for the first time and instantly feel better, as if you are basking in the warmth of the sun as soon as they smile or, conversely, if you feel nauseous and get the willies from the rancid vibes they are emitting after just one glance in their direction.

According to Nikola Tesla, "If you want to understand the Universe, think energy, frequency and vibration." Mr. Tesla was either highly intuitive or straight up psychic, based on his explanations of how his most innovative ideas came to him during visions that he knew to be something other than hallucinations. I'm not sure if he knew anything about auras and chakras, but both of them relate to energy and the wavelengths of colors which can affect a person's vibration. In order to keep your own energy balanced, or to help others do the same, I believe you must be at least somewhat familiar with each of these topics. I am providing a very brief introduction to each but suggest that you do some more extensive research and reading if you are interested in better educating yourself in the art of reading people's energy. Auras are the energy fields that radiate outside of our bodies, but these colorful vibes are a direct reflection of what is going on inside of you, within the seven energy centers known as chakras.

10 CHAKRAS 101

Understanding Internal Energy Centers

I'm a child of the 80s (one of Madonna's Material Girls), so when I began hearing from the dead, I didn't know a chakra from Chaka Khan. Turns out the seven chakras, or energy centers, are super important to everyone, especially those of us who muck around with energy from both sides of the veil. Because of this I had to learn a lot... and quickly! I originally put together this introduction in a blog post designed to give other newbies a basic understanding of what chakras are and how they work but have expanded upon it here. After reading this, and with a little practice, you should be able to recognize when one of your chakras gets wonky and at least attempt to do something about it.

You say CHA-kra, I say SHOCK-rah, same difference. Whichever pronunciation you adopt, the word chakra is Sanskrit for wheel, and I think that's the easiest way to picture them; seven spinning wheels running through the center of your body from the base of your tailbone to the top of your head. These energy centers are responsible for providing energy to every part of your mind, body and spirit. If one of them is spinning too fast or wobbling like one of the wheels on every ratchet shopping cart at Walmart, you will feel the effects either physically or emotionally. Each chakra corresponds to an area of the body and is associated with one of the colors in the ROY G BIV rainbow acronym. Each of them also has a fancy Sanskrit name in addition to the basic English names given here. I'm a language person and I still only remember half of the Sanskrit names, but feel free to be an overachiever and memorize both if you feel you must. I am far from an expert on chakras and I see no sense in reinventing the wheel (no pun intended) so, rather than insult the intelligence of the true gurus, I will give a brief explanation of each and then, once again, encourage you to read a book or two on the subject, do some online research, or head to your local New Age shop and pick up one of the handy dandy laminated "cheat sheets" that contain a concise (and nicely illustrated) explanation of all things chakra-related.

First up is the Root or Base Chakra, which (surprise!) is found at the base of your spine and is associated with the color red. This chakra's role is to connect all of your energy to the earth (or keep you "rooted"), which is called grounding. The root chakra is responsible for day-to-day survival (think financial and emotional stability), or the lowest level of Maslow's hierarchy of needs. For most people —but psychics, intuitives and empaths in particular— a failure to keep oneself grounded can lead to all kinds of emotional mayhem, with the end result usually being that you feel like a passenger on a plane that has been hijacked, overtaken by the overwhelming sense of despair that comes when your most basic needs are not met, even though all may be well with your wallet and your love life. The best way to straighten out this chakra (or any other) is through grounding. I believe grounding is the most important part of a psychic's spiritual health, so I'll go into detail and share some grounding tips further along in this section of the book. Psychics spend at least half of their time between worlds (with their head "in the clouds"), so it is imperative that we keep close tabs on this chakra. Whenever an overactive Root Chakra gets me feeling jittery or even spazzier than usual, I stop what I'm doing and head outside to ground, regardless of the weather conditions.

Located just below your navel (if you are a woman, it lines up with your uterus, or womb), is the second of your energy centers, known as the Sacral Chakra. This chakra is orange in color and associated with your identity, creativity and sexuality. If this chakra is balanced, you are able to enjoy the pleasurable things in life (good food, a glass of wine, sex) without overindulging and sliding down the slippery slopes of gluttony and addiction. Jenny Craig, Jack Daniels and the makers of methadone have made millions (and remain solvent) thanks to the overwhelming number of people skipping along with overactive sacral chakras in today's society. If this center is underactive, you might feel impotent, depressed or uninspired. Libido (sex drive) and fertility are also tied to this energy center. In addition to regular grounding, quick fixes for a wobbly second chakra include a night out painting pottery with friends or an evening of Netflix and chill, minus the Netflix (aka a booty call). I have long referred to sex as "Nature's Prozac" because of the wonders it has always done for my general sense of well-being and mental health. I'm not suggesting you go out and bang some rando every time you feel a bit uninspired, but I will never understand those who use sex as a bargaining chip, withholding it until some "honey-do" list is complete. In my opinion, you are just punishing yourself, and your third chakra, by denying yourself one of the few fabulous and FREE pleasures in life.

A bit further up (above your navel, below your ribs) lies the golden yellow Solar Plexus Chakra. This is the seat of your personal power and gives rise to what we call "gut instincts." I picture this chakra as a little ball of sunshine powering my self-confidence and wisdom. When something just doesn't feel right about a decision we've made, it's as if a cloud passes over that ball of sunshine, leaving us feeling uneasy, insecure or needy. On the flip side, when we get overconfident, greedy or controlling, it is a sign that this chakra has gone into overdrive. Issues with the digestive system or other internal organs can be attributed to an out of whack Solar Plexus Chakra. As a psychic, this is one of the spots where residual energy tends to clump up and get stuck. If I've had a super busy week with lots of readings and I forget to ground and do an "energy dump," messages don't come through as clearly and I can tell this chakra is blocked. The grounding cord meditation included later in one of the assigned activities literally works like Crystal Drano when this chakra gets clogged. Meditating and creating positive personal affirmations are also antidotes to your solar plexus woes.

The Heart Chakra is fourth in line and resides at the center of your breastbone. This green energy center powers everything associated with loving oneself and others. When all is well with this chakra, you are able to love yourself and others and handle any situation with kindness and compassion. When this green orb is spinning too fast you may feel (and behave) like a doormat or a victim, always on the giving end of love. You might also experience heartburn or a quickening of your pulse. Those who are emotionally unavailable or who have put up a wall, making it impossible to connect with them on any real level are suffering from an underactive heart chakra, most likely due to a lack of love or some other trauma early in life. This energy center is also associated with health and healing, and you can harness its power (and help balance your own) by doing something nice for yourself or someone else. Psychics can receive a lot of information through this chakra, as well as the three above it. To make any true spiritual progress, you must always work towards healing and opening this chakra, releasing any past traumas in order to fully love yourself and others. This means making peace with and letting go of past anger and resentment. If you are a dweller by nature, you may have your work cut out for you. It's much harder (near impossible) to free your mind and spirit enough to communicate with Spirit if you are harboring a well of past ills in this chakra.

Moving on up the ladder we come to the fifth energy center, aka the Throat chakra. I won't insult your intelligence by telling you where it's located. As you might have also guessed, it is the powerhouse behind our ability to communicate freely. When this chakra is functioning properly, you will feel as if you somehow know just the right thing to say, and that your words are heard by and of benefit to others. A slack throat chakra can lead to feelings of not being heard, or an inability to speak your personal truth with confidence and clarity. If you've ever run into someone who just loves to hear themselves speak or, if you do get a word in edgewise, never really hears what you are saying because they are too busy thinking of what they are going to say next, you've witnessed how a dysfunctional throat chakra can manifest itself. A psychic's clairaudience can be affected by a blockage of this chakra as well. If I hear a near constant (and maddening) buzzing, chirping or dull ringing (aka tinnitus) in one or both ears, I know that this wheel needs a realignment. A good cry or singing your heart out in the car or shower can help clear this energy center.

Speaking of songs, when I hear the lyrics, "Run, run, run, run wide open, are you electrified is your third eye open?" from Arthur Buck's song "Are You Electrified" I know immediately to pop the hood and take a look at my sixth chakra. The Third Eye is probably the most well-recognized or mainstream of the chakras. It's usually represented as a huge henna-fied indigo eyeball resting between your eyebrows. For this reason, it is also commonly known as the Brow Chakra. Activating this chakra opens us to the mysteries and magic of the psychic world. When this chakra is activated and energy is flowing freely through it, you will be open to receiving information beyond what your five senses pick up using your new friends, the Clairs. As mysterious and elusive as opening this chakra may seem, there is actually a small, pinecone-shaped gland in your brain —the pineal gland— that takes in light and regulates your waking and sleeping patterns. Many cultures believe that activating the pineal gland beyond this basic function is the secret to opening the Third Eye. Not surprisingly, when you begin to awaken spiritually, you will more than likely begin awakening in the wee hours of the night. This is because when you are resting peacefully, disconnected from the demands of the everyday world, folks in the Spirit World see this as the perfect opportunity to connect and enlighten you. Unless your psychic abilities are very developed or you spend the majority of your time messing with hobbies like tarot cards and ghost hunting, you probably don't need to worry about your third eye being overactive. When I hear the song I mentioned earlier, or feel like I'm unable to focus on what's going on in the real world (e.g. my husband thinks I'm ignoring him, but I am actually just incapable of tuning out the Other Side), I make a concerted effort to shut the curtains on this window to the Other Side. Connecting with the Earth by grounding is the best way to save yourself (and your relationships) from the pitfalls of being too "woke."

The seventh and last energy center is the Crown chakra and, just like the tiaras found among the queen's crown jewels, it perches at the very top of your head. It is associated with the most royal of colors as well, violet (or purple if you prefer), and connects us to the entire Universe. This is the first chakra that I *knew* I was receiving information from. The top of my head would tingle as if I were wearing a tinfoil hat too close to an old-fashioned television antenna and then I would see or hear someone who wasn't actually there (a spirit or discarnate entity). The only reason I even knew about my crown chakra and figured out what was going on was that the psychic I mentioned earlier had told me that this was going to happen. I was hesitant to believe him but, once again, he was right on the money. It wasn't until I started studying everything that I could about being psychic that I began to understand that I was seeing things thanks to my third eye chakra or hearing things thanks to my throat chakra. There is no such thing as an overactive crown chakra, and an underactive one simply means you are a "normal" human being.

HOMEWORK ASSIGNMENT #2
Opening Your Chakras

Keeping all of your chakras healthy and balanced is important for anyone, but for most of you, opening and activating the last four chakras mentioned is the key to interfacing with the universe, which is probably your aim in reading this book. In order to effectively do a reading (we call it a reading because you are reading someone's energy), you must open up these last four chakras. Whether your ultimate goal is to do readings or simply to develop your psychic powers and intuition to better understand and improve yourself, you will need to do the same in order to open up and tune into your Guides and the Universe. Here are a few quick ways to make sure that these four chakras are open, starting with the heart chakra. Find a quiet spot and give each of the visualizations (2A-D) below a whirl.

2A Opening Your Heart Chakra

I always make sure to open my heart chakra before a reading so that I am sure to be sending and receiving love freely during any interaction I have with those on this side and the other.

If I am having a hard time reading someone because they are nervous, skeptical or just your average Cancer or Scorpio with a built-in tough exterior auric shell, I ask them to close their eyes and lead them through it as well.

Close your eyes, take a deep breath, and imagine an unopened rosebud in the center of your chest. As you exhale, imagine the green leaves of the rosebud unfurling, and a beautiful pink rose beginning to blossom. Take another deep breath, saying to yourself "I am open to giving and receiving love from the Universe." As you exhale this time, imagine the rose opening to a full bloom.

2B Opening Your Throat Chakra

I'm a talker and don't generally have difficulty expressing myself, so I don't purposefully do anything to open this chakra before every reading, but if you need to, try this:

Go somewhere that you can sing loudly and without inhibition (the shower, your car, or wherever it is that you can do so without embarrassing yourself or destroying anyone's hearing). Pick a song, anything upbeat and happy that you love to sing-along with will do. Play it as loud as comfort allows and let 'er rip.

Because clairaudience is also connected to this chakra, you may have to open your ears as well. If your ears feel blocked (if sounds seem more muffled than usual or they feel like they need to be popped), try visualizing corks in each ear and then imagine pulling them out.

2C Opening Your Third Eye Chakra

This one can be a little trickier, but I believe that with practice, anyone can do it. As a psychic I tend to see things whether I choose to or not, but if my clairvoyance seems a little low and I am not "seeing" as much as usual when tuned in, I do the following.

Close your eyes and imagine a window between your eyebrows. Imagine that the curtains are drawn on this window. Visualize the curtains on this window slowly opening. once the curtains are completely open, you see that the window has two panes that swing open from the center like doors. Undo the latch at the center of the window and push the two panes open as wide as you can, until you can see the night sky, which is indigo and filled with all the stars in the universe.

2D Opening Your Crown Chakra

By opening this Chakra, you are in essence sending out a signal to the Universe, letting the Other Side know that you are "open for business".

Close your eyes and imagine the there is a little lighthouse perched on the top of your head. You are at the top of the lighthouse looking out of the huge windows and can see the vast, indigo night sky full of stars, but no one can yet see you. To your left is a big switch. You flip this switch on, sending a bright spotlight out into the night sky, allowing travelers from the Spiritnet to recognize and communicate with you.

HOMEWORK ASSIGNMENT #3

Closing Your Chakras
(Tuning Out and Closing Up Shop)

This topic may seem counterintuitive to the goal of this book, which is to assist you in *opening* these energy centers so that you can tune in, but if you succeed in doing so to the level of using them full-time, it is inevitable that at some point you will feel bombarded by downloads from the Spiritnet. If and when this happens, no matter how tough and resourceful your Gatekeeper is, you need to be able to lend a hand by intentionally turning the Spirit cable box off. Remember the old saying, "There's more than one way to skin a cat"? Well, there's more than one way to shut down this circuit as well. I'll share a few that I have either picked up from others along the way or been shown by my own Guides. These are especially helpful at night, when you are trying to sleep and can't figure out how to tune out for the evening. I recommend trying each on for size to see what suits you best, as well as keeping your Third Eye open to any suggestions from your own Guides.

3A Closing Your Crown Chakra

These little techniques are brought to you by my Guides, God love them, who struggled so hard to teach me to *not* leave the light on 24/7. I use one of these tricks whenever I can't relax or sleep, because someone is knocking on the door to my Crown Chakra with the persistence of a woodpecker.

1. *Close your eyes and imagine a bright, naked lightbulb at the top of your head. Shield your eyes a bit and imagine yourself reaching up, pulling the string attached to the fixture, and turning the light off.*

2. *Close your eyes and imagine your head being encased in a birdcage. Now imagine a blanket being draped over the birdcage, blocking any light from entering through the crown of your head. Adjust the blanket until the cage is completely covered and it is completely dark underneath, or until the "tweeting" (annoyance) stops and your mind is quiet.*

3. *Close your eyes and imagine an open manhole at the top of your head. You see a huge spotlight coming in through the open hole, the light from which is blinding. Imagine a helpful workman (your Gatekeeper) coming along and dragging a heavy lid over the hole until it is completely covered and so dark inside of your head that you can't see anything at all.*

3B Closing Your Third Eye Chakra

Remember that big window you visualized while opening your Third Eye? If you can't seem to shut down the random images that can at times flood any psychic thanks to an open sixth chakra, try this.

Close your eyes and imagine a big window between your brows. You notice that the two window panes are flung wide open and the curtains are flapping loudly in the wind. Reach out and pull both panes shut. Be sure to securely fasten the latch in the middle. Pull the curtains closed, making sure you haven't left any cracks where the light can enter.

3C Closing Your Throat Chakra

If you are trying to sleep, only to be annoyed by random

frequencies, buzzing or popping sounds in one or both ears, try this quick fix:

Close your eyes and imagine a cork hanging by a string from each of your ears. Now imagine some helpful little sprite like Tinkerbell coming along and gently pushing the corks into each ear, blocking out all sound.

HOMEWORK ASSIGNMENT #4

Regulating the Flow of Energy and Information

Once you are receiving information regularly from the universe, you may feel the need to dial things up or down a bit as needed. This is also an excellent tool for anyone, psychic or not, who struggles with being overstimulated and/or overwhelmed in crowded or loud spaces.

Close your eyes and picture a wall in front of you. Now imagine an old school dial in the middle of the wall. The bottom left of the dial says "OFF" and the bottom right says "ON". If you want to dial back or completely turn off the energy flow/the amount of information you are receiving, turn the dial to the left. To open up the flow a bit, turn the dial to the right.

Helpful Hint: If you want to avoid a Spirit "mob scene" (and a headache), it is probably wise to never dial up the flow to more than 75-80% capacity.

11 AS THE WHEEL TURNS

Checking and Balancing Your Chakras

Now that you've acquired a basic understanding of the seven chakras, you're ready to start assessing these energy centers and rebalancing them as needed. Just as your car tires need occasional balancing and realignment, so do your chakras. Are you someone who is somewhat lethargic and can't function without coffee, or do you pretty much bounce off the walls as soon as your feet hit the floor? Anyone who has met me would probably agree that I have what my husband lovingly refers to as spazzy energy. This is both a blessing and a curse. It is a blessing in that Spirit work requires a lot of energy and spirits themselves are attracted to it; it is a curse when it attracts the wrong kind of energy.

Most of the time I know that Spirit is trying to align itself with me in order to communicate through me because of the telltale tingles I have discussed. Sometimes I get a huge chill and I know that someone from the Other Side is invading my space in order to experience something in the physical world that they miss since becoming discarnate (without a physical body). Other times I get too wound up and my vibration runs too high, like a fever, weakening my spiritual defenses and leaving me susceptible to unearthly "ills." In any of these cases, whenever I leave myself wide open to the Spirit World, there is always the potential for other rogue energies to invade, and things get jacked up for me on the receiving end. When this happens, my Guides usually show me my crown chakra as a lighthouse beacon sending a signal a bit too far and wide, so I know that I need to dial it down through grounding, meditation, or one of the little tricks that I shared earlier. As an empath, I also often feel whatever others around me are feeling, so I always do a quick "chakra run" or check before each reading that I do to make sure the problem is theirs as opposed to mine. I use what I call "Beth's Basic Meditation" because it is my go-to, all-purpose meditation. I consider it one-stop shopping because in less than three minutes it allows you to protect yourself, raise your vibration, and check that your chakras are running smoothly and open to receiving. I put this meditation in writing in the assignment box below to make it easier to find later on when it is needed in conjunction with the other guided activities and assignments that involve tuning in. You may find it useful to listen to it rather than read it, at least until you become better acquainted with it and can do it on your own. The recorded version can be accessed on my website.

HOMEWORK ASSIGNMENT #5

Protect, Check & Raise Your Vibration

BETH'S BASIC MEDITATION
Get a bookmark or fold the corner of this page, because I'll be sending you back here before just about every other suggested homework assignment that follows. In addition to being printed here, it can be accessed as a recording on the *Psychic Development Resources* page of my website: **bethparkermedium.com**

Step 1: Protect and ground yourself
Sit comfortably but pay attention to your posture. Imagine a golden cord attached to the top of your head, pulling you up straight so that your spine and chakras are straight and aligned. Close your eyes, take a long deep cleansing breath and imagine sparkly white plus signs entering your body, bringing you positive energy. Slowly breath out, and picture dull, gray minus signs leaving your body, releasing any old, crusty or negative energy. Inhale again, taking another deep cleansing breath, drawing in sparkly positive energy... and exhale... releasing all negative energy to be absorbed back into the Earth.

Imagine a beautiful bright blue sky with fluffy white clouds. imagine a magical golden white light streaming down from the clouds, beaming directly onto you, and surrounding your entire body like a bright, warm, safe cocoon. You can see the bright light outlining your body and you feel warm and protected. Say to yourself "I encircle myself in the white light of

God's love and divine protection". Now imagine a cord of that protective white light forming at the base of your spine and attaching itself to the Earth. You feel secure, calm and grounded. You are ready to open your chakras and raise your vibration to connect with your higher self and your Guides.

Step 2: Open your chakras
Now imagine that same bright golden white light entering your root chakra. You see the red orb at the base of your spine getting brighter and start to spin like a top as it gathers energy from the white light. As soon as you sense the red orb spinning, the light moves upward and enters your sacral chakra. You watch as the orange orb just below you belly button gets brighter and starts spinning. Once it is spinning, the light moves up to your solar plexus. When the yellow orb at your center glows brighter and begins to spin, the light also gains energy and moves up to your heart chakra. You see the bright green heart in the center of your chest swell, get brighter, and start spinning. This sends light and love outward signaling that your heart is open to giving and receiving, before moving upwards, to your throat chakra. The bright blue orb in your throat gets brighter, picks up energy, and begins to spin. This energy helps you to hear and communicate clearly and helps power the light up to the indigo orb between your eyebrows. As your third eye chakra becomes brighter and begins to spin, you are open to see clearly. You follow the light as it flows up to the violet orb that is your crown chakra. As the violet orb gets brighter and begins to spin, it opens up, so that the magical, luminous light flows out of your body and forms a golden white funnel, which opens you up to communicate with and receive wisdom from your Guides and the Universe.

Note: The first time I suggest just reading (or listening) to get your bearings. The next time, pay closer attention to each spinning orb and see if any of them appears to flash like a blinking traffic light, is spinning noticeably faster or slower than the others, or seems to wobble. This is your cue that something is out of whack.

Meditation takes many forms. Most people who have never meditated picture someone in desperate need of a haircut sitting in the traditional pretzel-legged lotus position and chanting "Om". I'm much more comfortable sitting in a chair, with my feet planted on the ground, especially during my morning meditation when I need to be able to tune in *and* take notes from Spirit on my iPad. A peaceful walk in nature or an early morning jog are forms of meditation for some. Anything that allows you to quiet the mind and be present in the moment will do. Whether or not you decide to incorporate my basic meditation (or another of your choosing) into your daily repertoire, the long-term benefits of this practice are impossible to ignore. When I began teaching, I was diagnosed with ADD; first by my brutally honest students, then by an actual doctor. I used Adderall for years to stay focused, but I no longer need it thanks to my newfound awareness and the tools that I've shared here. I do not shun modern medicine and I'm not telling you to dump the meds if they are working for you —I'll never forget the first time I took them for ADD and realized how a "normal"/non-spazzy brain functions... it was a truly magical moment— but I am living proof that you can achieve the same focus through an awareness of your chakras, meditation, and other centering and grounding activities that I will be sharing with you. Please don't stress out if you are still a tad confused (or completely lost) when it comes to checking your chakras after this brief intro. You can at least recognize when you are dog tired for no apparent reason or just feeling kind of mental, right? When this happens, go back and re-read the suggestions provided under each chakra. If you sense that something may be seriously unbalanced, or you want to try something new, I recommend finding an energy practitioner in your area. A good Reiki session is like a massage for the soul!

12 ENERGY BOOSTING AND BALANCING

Spiritual Health Habits

Whether you are a natural empath who has always been affected by any energy that you come into contact with, or have only just begun to notice a heightened sensitivity to other energies as a side effect of opening up to the Spirit World, you need to learn to recognize and separate your own energy from that of others, whose energy may be intrusive or unhealthy. As a medium, I am in the business of opening my energy field to the energy of others both here and on the Other Side, alas (in the interest of saving my own sanity), I have had to learn how to recognize whether a sudden burst of euphoria or mini meltdown is my own or possibly attached to the person coming for a reading later in the day.

Although I'm an extrovert and one of those people who have never met a stranger, I'm also a homebody and have always preferred to stay in after work because being in crowds or around certain people makes me cranky and out of sorts. Being a teacher and a mother I had to learn to tune out a lot of background noise, and I felt at home in a classroom of thirty students, but when I took over as the advisor for our Student Government Association, I absolutely loathed the pep rallies where the entire school would gather in one big mob. I looked forward to interacting with my colleagues and students each day, but I always required a good stretch of quiet alone time once I got home. I could probably count on one hand the number of times per year I went to happy hour or any other after-hours function. If any of this resonates with you, if you sometimes just feel cruddy after having too much contact with the world at large, or start to feel drained or deflated like a flat tire once you start connecting with other energies in the Universe, you are more than likely an empath. There are many ways to dump lingering stale or crusty energy and feel lighter and better in general without counting calories or dusting off your scale.

The tips and tricks in this next section have made a huge impact on my life. I call them *5-Minute Fixes* and have gotten a lot of positive feedback when I've shared them on social media. I believe they will benefit you as well if you make them habits. Each is designed to raise your vibration or help you to put out good vibes, both of which act as natural repellents against the crusty vibes that exist on both sides of the veil. Consider them vitamin C or bug spray for the soul. You may have noticed that energy vampires —those negative creatures that do nothing but complain or create drama in your daily habitat— keep their distance from the positive peppy types. This is no coincidence. Incorporate a few (or all) of these practices into your daily routine and you'll be able to leave the human flyswatter at home because your new and improved auric field will do the job for you.

HOMEWORK ASSIGNMENT #6

Adopt an Attitude of Gratitude

The single most important thing you can do to raise your vibration and improve your daily life forever is to focus on the positive and give thanks for all of the good things in your life, be they big or small… no matter how crappy you might feel.

- *Begin and end each day by giving thanks for all that is good or going well in your life.*

- *If you are not facing major issues and things are generally going your way, a simple "Thank you, God, Guides, Universe (or whomever and whatever you pray or give cred to) for the gift of this day and past days, and for the possibility of the future", should suffice. I personally take time to thank God, Jesus, Mary and Joseph, The Saints, my Guides, relatives past & present (basically anyone who may be listening), but you do you. Whatever you are comfortable with is just fine.*

- *Giving thanks is even more important when things are not going your way, because it has a greater impact on your mental state and the day ahead. In this case, I suggest something along the lines of "Thank you, God, Guides, Universe (or whomever) for the gift of this day. I know that whatever difficulties I am experiencing are temporary and meant to teach me something and help me grow. I appreciate this opportunity and have faith that you will help me to overcome this and create something positive out of my current life challenge."*

- *End each day by giving thanks as well. If the day was a bit of a struggle, try asking your Guides to help you find the meaning of what you have gone through while you sleep. Jot down anything you remember experiencing in the dream state as soon as you wake up. You may just find hidden answers in what you would have previously considered a random dream or nightmare once you are fully awake and lucid.*

HOMEWORK ASSIGNMENT #7

Create an Energy Playlist and Listen to it Regularly

Nothing raises your vibration like music. It doesn't matter what kind it is, so long as it boosts your energy and makes you feel better. I have created several different energy playlists and they never fail to boost my mood. For me it's not always about the lyrics. Some might consider most of Eminem's lyrics to contain less than positive messages, but when I don't feel like getting on the elliptical at 6am, nothing gets me motivated like Mr. Mather's hits, "Lose Yourself" or "WTP" (White Trash Party). If I am a little down or feel the need to bring out my inner goddess, I cue up Aretha Franklin's "RESPECT", or one of Meghan Trainor's modern songs of empowerment.

Make a list of any songs that make you feel happy or that you can't help but sing along to. Create a playlist on your phone or keep a stack of old school records, cassettes or CDs in a handy spot and listen to them regularly. Pay attention to how you are feeling before and after even five or ten minutes of this energy boosting fix.

BONUS: The Spirit World loves music as much as we do and will be highly attracted to the vibes being put out. Since becoming a medium, I am rarely alone when I listen to music; especially when I exercise. Within 5 minutes of cranking up the tunes my head usually starts tingling and I am joined by my Guides or whoever's loved ones happen to be waiting in the wings for my next reading.

HOMEWORK ASSIGNMENT #8

Move Your Body

You don't have to be an athlete or run five miles a day to benefit from the vibe boosting power of physical activity. I'm a huge fan of Richard Simmons (I lost all of my baby weight in the 90's thanks to *Deal-a-Meal* and *Sweatin' to the Oldies*), but the goal of this assignment is not weight loss; it is to make you feel lighter from the inside out. Any movement that you can sustain for five or ten minutes (or more) can accomplish this when your body and soul are feeling a bit sluggish or heavy. I highly recommend incorporating music into whichever activity you choose, for an extra boost.

Choose one of the activities below and set a timer for 5 minutes. Sit (or stand) still and take 3 deep cleansing breaths. In between each breath say to yourself "I am doing this for me, because my body and soul deserve it."

Press start on the timer and bust a move!

- Dance. *Find a private spot, cue up your energy playlist and get into the groove.*

- Walk or skip, *outside if possible or around the house or office if not.*

- Stretch every part of your body. *I do 5-10 minutes of "faux yoga" first thing every morning. I call it faux because I've never attended an actual yoga class and I got all of my moves off of boxes of Yogi Tea.*

If you need a little extra motivation, request a little help from your Guides during your morning meditation or just before you get moving. Even if you can't *see* them like I do, I'm willing to bet that you will feel a difference in your overall drive and stamina. You may enjoy this mini boost so much that you find yourself ignoring the alarm on the timer you set and moving a bit more!

HOMEWORK ASSIGNMENT #9

Do Something Nice for Someone Else

A lot of you reading this are probably natural givers and do this all the time, without giving it a second thought, but I believe that doing it with intention brings on even more good karma. Random Acts of Kindness have been around since the early 80s, thanks to Anne Herbert, who wrote the phrase on a placemat and then turned it into a book. The Pay it Forward movement came later, but the gist is the same; do something unexpectedly kind for someone. I'm a firm believer in what goes around comes around (aka the boomerang effect) but doing something kind just for the hell of it makes you feel good and raises your vibration instantly, whether you ever experience a tangible payback or not. There is no shortage of ideas online, but I've made the following activities as simple and painless as possible, so that not even the most hardcore slacker can whine about not having the time.

- *Stop reading, take two minutes and try one or more of the following suggestions.*

- *If you have a loved one nearby, tell them you love them. If you are alone, send an "I love you" text to someone. If you aren't comfortable with the "L" word, send a text telling someone that you are glad they are in your life. Extra credit if you add a reason why.*

- *Give someone a compliment. If you are alone, text someone a compliment.*

- *If you are alone, have no phone, it is late at night or you are stranded on a desert island with nothing but a soccer ball named Wilson, simply close your eyes, think of someone and send a silent "I love you" or some other compliment their way telepathically.*

Note: I use this last little trick all of the time with people that I don't actually like. As soon as a negative thought about them creeps into my head, I picture them, force myself to think of something nice, and mentally send the positive thought their way. This is not always easy, but you can totally train your brain to help you fight any negativity that tries to weasel its way in.

The last set of activities was designed to help you create good vibes and keep them going throughout the day. The next set will help you to protect the positive vibes you've got flowing once you've left your happy place —whatever soul sanctuary you have created for yourself— and are at the mercy of any irksome energy that you may encounter. Before moving on, however, I feel it is important to mention the need to pay attention to environmental factors that can lower your vibration, especially now that you are making a concerted effort to raise it. In addition to the *Big Two* (drugs and alcohol), the dangers of which I covered at length earlier, there are other habits that you should consider curbing as well, like junk food. My diet is still far from "clean" by health nut standards, but I have come a long way since the days when I would fall asleep eating sweets and wake up with a Fun Dip candy stick stuck to my thigh. You might try limiting your exposure to the news and social media as well. I'm not saying that you need to go through life uninformed or completely out of touch with the world of fakebook, but if you find your blood pressure rising over the things you are seeing on the boob tube or online, doesn't it make sense to turn off, unfollow or block the shows and feeds that make you go apoplectic? You can throw up energy shields left and right, but you'll have less need for them if you avoid things that you instinctively know bring you down.

HOMEWORK ASSIGNMENT #10

Create an Energy Shield of Armor

These handy little visualizations are similar to those I shared earlier and can be used every day before work, school, or anytime you'll be around a crowd of potentially negative or crazy town energy. The object here is to place an added buffer around your auric energy field as you wage daily war against any murky or suspect energy.

Close your eyes and envision a shield of white light encasing your body like a suit of armor that is capable of protecting you from any negative energy. Now rub your hands together to create a ball of energy between them (rub until the warmth of the softball-shaped energy you have created is palpable when you separate your hands). Slowly wave your hands in front of you, creating an added shield or barrier between you and any encroaching energy. It may sound a little kooky, but don't knock it 'til you try it.

HOMEWORK ASSIGNMENT #11

Reclaim Your Energy

Gasoline is the energy that we use to fuel our cars. When your car runs out of gas, you head to the station to fill it back up. This activity is designed to do the same for your own energy tank, making sure that it remains topped off, especially when you are feeling drained at the end of the day. I do this faithfully after every reading, even when all of the energy that I encounter is positive, because I put so much of my own personal reserves into these exchanges. If you are new to energy work or expend a lot of emotional energy in your current profession, I recommend doing this at the end of each day, either in your car during your commute, or as soon as you get home.

- *Close your eyes (unless you are driving) and imagine all of the people you came into contact with/used your energy on that day, especially those who have drained your energy rather than boosting it.*

- *Open your heart chakra (remember the blooming pink rose activity?)*

- *Mentally send positive vibes —in the form of hearts, a rainbow, magical sparkly dust or rose petals… whatever works— to that group of people you just imagined.*

- *Picture that energy coming back out of the tops of their heads, cycling through the clouds high above (like a heavenly rinse cycle), and then re-entering your body as fresh, clean energy through the crown of your head.*

Note: If you only encounter a few people daily or prefer to focus on the one or two that were particularly draining, you can do this for each one as opposed to a mass of coworkers, students or what have you.

HOMEWORK ASSIGNMENT #12

Recharge with Daily Grounding

I mentioned the importance of grounding several times in relation to chakras, and now is the moment you've all been waiting for. Grab a highlighter or a sticky tab, because this next habit is the key to staying sane once you have opened up to the Spirit World. Anyone can benefit from grounding but is absolutely essential to empaths and psychics. It essentially involves connecting with the Earth in some way in order to re-center yourself, dump any old energy, and recharge. I practice this at least once a day and I try not to rush through it or cut corners. The effects of this ritual are so noticeable that anytime I start acting weirder than usual, my husband is quick to ask if I've forgotten to ground.

Do this once daily, preferably after work or sometime before going to bed.

- *Take your shoes off and lay down (or stand) in the grass or sand. If it's too wet or cold, you can do this inside while holding a palm-sized basic rock that you dig up and bring in from outside.*

- *Imagine that magical white light from the clouds (the one I mentioned earlier) beaming down and creating a cocoon around your entire body. Imagine your feet growing roots and connecting you to the ground. Next envision a golden cord attached to your root chakra (that red ball of energy at the base of your spine). In your mind's eye, connect that cord to the ground, like an anchor forming out of the white light surrounding you.*

- *Take 3-4 deep breaths. Each time you breathe in, imagine white sparkly plus signs (positive energy) entering your entire body. Each time you exhale, imagine grey minus signs (negative energy) leaving your body through that golden cord and going into the earth where it will be neutralized and recycled.*

- *If you have any persistent negative thoughts (a worry or a person that you can't stop thinking about), imagine them in a thought bubble, pop that bubble and watch as the "ashes" of that thought exit through your golden cord.*

BONUS/GROUNDING BOOSTER: Get yourself a small citrine crystal (found in any new age store or on Amazon), which is known for its amazing grounding properties. Place it on your solar plexus while you are grounding if you are able to lay down.

HOMEWORK ASSIGNMENT #13

Super Deluxe Grounding

I discovered this grounding cord meditation after I had a past life regression done by a local hypnotherapist, Carly Ptak. I was so impressed that I went to her website and downloaded all of the amazing FREE resources that she has recorded and gifted the Universe with. I call this the "Super Dump & Recharge" and do it weekly or whenever I feel especially heavy or crusty.

Go to www.integrationhypnotherapy.com, click on Hypnosis Mp3 Downloads, scroll down and click on the Grounding Cord link. A link to this website can also be found on the Psychic Development Resources page of my website. Put in some earbuds, press play, close your eyes, and be prepared to feel like a huge weight has been lifted from you in under ten minutes. You're welcome!

P.S. My husband and I have both done past life regressions with Carly and it was super cool. She offers them in person or via an online conferencing system and I definitely recommend adding this experience to your bucket list.

HOMEWORK ASSIGNMENT #14

Home Energy Cleanse

I cleanse our house daily with an incense stick (frankincense and myrrh is my fave), but you should at the very least do it when you can't seem to shake the negative energy, or if it feels like you are surrounded by a dark cloud as soon you walk in the door. If your pets start acting weird or refuse to go into a certain area of the house, that's another good indication that the energy is "off" and the space needs a good spiritual cleansing.

- *Get some sage, incense or palo santo sticks, a receptacle for the ashes and a lighter.*

- *Open at least one window in every room.*

- *Light the sage or incense and slowly walk through the house, wafting it through every room. Pay special attention to the corners and any dark crawl spaces or basement areas.*

- *Optional (but not necessary): Repeat (either to yourself or aloud) a positive affirmation such as "I release and banish all negative energy from this space. I welcome fresh new energy in its place."*

NOTE: Sometimes there is an actual toxic person who makes the energy less than palatable where you live, in which case you may not be able to rid yourself of them (at least not immediately). You can, however, rid your personal space of their nasty vibes with this technique!

    Whether you choose to begin doing one, a few or all of the suggested energy-related activities that I shared, I'm willing to bet that you will start to feel the difference almost immediately as I did. Diet and exercise certainly help us to feel lighter physically, however if, like me, you want to start feeling better without totally giving up your poison of choice, becoming more aware of the effect that the intangible energy surrounding you may be having on your mental and emotional health will help you to put a finger on why else you may not be "feeling yourself". Once you recognize what (or who) may be draining you of energy, the better you will get at managing your energy field and tuning out any energy that may be distracting or wearing you down. It's a bit like adjusting the radio when the station gets staticky; the better able you are to control the dial, the less funky or "staticky" your personal station will feel.

PART III:

TOOLS OF THE TRADE

BOOSTING YOUR CONNECTION TO THE SPIRITNET

There are many tools that you can use to help boost your connection to the Universe. From early childhood on I have been drawn to all things New Age. I have dabbled in Astrology, Numerology, Tarot, Rune Stones and more. I think it is important to familiarize yourself with several of them and then choose one or two to really sink your teeth into in order to boost your connection to the Spiritnet and speed up your progress. I have chosen to introduce you to a few that I am most familiar with and partial to, but this does not mean they are superior to any of the other myriad tools out there. Some of the things that I am about to share may work better (lead to more "Eureka!" and "Aha!" moments) for you than others. My guess is that your Guides will take full advantage of what you read here because they create so many of what we educators call "teachable moments." Homework assignments will follow each introduction; you can take the teacher out of school, but you can't the school out of the teacher... sorry, not sorry!

HOMEWORK ASSIGNMENT #15

Prepare Your Psychic Homeschool Classroom

You'll need a quiet space and a few "school supplies" to get started on your DIY psychic journey. You don't need an entire room… any cozy corner will do. I started out on the living room sofa, before banishing my husband's weights to the basement and setting up shop in our den. I eventually settled in the official Reading Room that I prepared upstairs when my hobby turned into a career and I needed a legit space to welcome clients. Add a candle (or two or three) and anything else that calms or inspires you. If you are short on space, you can dedicate one shelf on your bookcase, or keep your sacred meditation objects on a tray that can be easily stowed away and pulled back out as needed. I now have a mobile meditation altar (a gold and glass drinks tray on wheels) that I roll in and out of my Reading Room to make more space for clients. In addition to candles, incense, and crystals, mine is full of things that are meaningful only to me —prayer cards, my dad's favorite mug, my favorite Barbie from childhood— tbh it pretty much resembles a Day of the Dead offrenda or a shrine set up by a stalker in some creepy horror film.

- *Set up your sacred space as described above.*

- *Get yourself a notebook or journal and whatever writing utensil you prefer. I chose sparkly composition books because I think glitter is magical and they are portable. They don't have to be* fancy. I've made a couple of cracks about Walmart in this book, but if it weren't for Sam Walton (the genius who brought bulk prices to the masses) and the Power of Prime, my journal and candle budget would've broken the bank by now.

- Dedicate a minimum of 30 minutes each day to your development practices and try to do it around the same time if possible. I've always been an early-to-bed-early-to-rise person (my parents literally never had to tell me it was time for bed), so I do the majority of my daily meditating and tuning in between 4 and 6am, before the rest of the house is awake, but if you're a night owl, you might prefer 11pm or later, once the rest of the house is asleep. You'll get the most out of it if you work with, rather than against, your own natural biorhythms.

HOMEWORK ASSIGNMENT #16

Journal Entry #1

Have you had any previous psychic or paranormal experiences? If so, take some time to jot them down in your journal. If you are able, make note of your age at the time and any significant events in your life that may have occurred around the same time. Keep your journal handy and continue to record anything exciting or new that occurs once you begin tuning in!

HOMEWORK ASSIGNMENT #17

Energy Reading with Candles

Hopefully by now you have become more attuned to the subtle shifts in energy that you may have previously ignored or taken for granted. One surefire way to gauge how much energy is present is by lighting a candle (or several) in a controlled environment and observing how the flames dance in response to each shift in energy. I'm no pyro, but I've always been mesmerized by a good bonfire and have been reading flames for years. I have several candles set up for this purpose on my morning meditation altar, and I have four others that I use during readings so that clients can see how the energy in the room ebbs and flows according to who is visiting from the Spirit World. I also encourage them to do the following activity when they get home so that they can get a more concrete visual confirmation of the presence of the energy of their deceased loved ones when they attempt to communicate with them.

- *You only need one candle, but I think it's useful to have two or more of the same kind so that you can compare how differently they behave.*

- *Set your candle(s) up in a peaceful room with no windows open and away from any direct air vents that might interfere with getting a clean read of the energy present.*

- *Light the candle(s) and say the basic protection prayer that you memorized or created for yourself earlier.*

- *Start a conversation with someone in the Spirit World (either a deceased loved one or your Spirit Guides). Ask specific questions or just chat as if they were there. If the candles are not in a protective glass container, be sure that you are sitting far enough away that your breath is not affecting the flames.*

- *Change your tone of voice and watch as the flame(s) react. Sometimes they will appear to do a happy dance, sometimes they will spike sharply upward, other times they will be still and quiet. It's also interesting to turn on different kinds of music and note how the flames react to each.*

This activity can also be used to gauge the energy of anyone physically present in the house. Experiment by moving your candles to other areas and watch what happens as the energy of different living people affects them. The flames will behave differently around your bookworm sister than they do in the presence of your live wire little brother.

13 AUTOMATIC WRITING 101

Get Your John Nash On

I'm starting with this tool because it was absolutely crucial to my development as a psychic medium. Automatic Writing, aka Psychography, is the psychic ability that allows a person to create written words without consciously writing. This doesn't mean that you close your eyes and let the pen roll across the paper willy nilly. It basically involves asking your Guides or the Universe a question, clearing your mind, tuning in and scribbling down anything that comes to you without "thinking". When I do it each morning, it's as if I am tuning in, listening and taking dictation. I write down not only what I hear, but anything that I see, sense or feel as well. As I've said before, it may seem strange or difficult to separate your own thoughts from direct downloads from the Spiritnet but, like any skill, it gets easier and more natural with practice. The experience can vary greatly from one person to the next, but here's how it usually works for me. Although much of the psychic information that I receive comes in the form of a voice that I hear, it never sounds like my own voice, and is often preceded by a physically sensation such as a tingling, a random twitch or pulse, or a high frequency in one hear that lets me know to pay attention. It does take a while to trust these voices, but once you get the hang of it (and are able to validate the predictions or personal information provided), you can begin to relax and embrace these messages as gifts from the Universe… and no longer worry that they are a symptom of schizophrenia or some other mental illness!

Once I began receiving messages from the Spirit World on a fairly regular basis, I began recording them in one of my many sparkly composition books. At the time I did this because I received most of my messages from the Other Side during my morning meditation sessions and they were often too long for me to recall when I went to deliver them to the intended recipient. I soon realized how valuable this was for other purposes as well. I now had a record of *everything* that I received from Spirit, which meant that if part of a message didn't "fit", I could look back at everything that I had written and further discern between what I was receiving from someone's deceased family members versus what was being given to me psychically from my Guides or other sources in the Spiritnet. For the first year or more I dragged my sparkly journal everywhere so that I could record anything that I received throughout the day, as well as any synchronicities which were too great to ignore. By the time I decided to quit my day job and work with Spirit full-time, I had close to forty sparkly journals. My husband teasingly calls them the John Nash notebooks because they appear to be filled with mad scribblings and sketches similar to those covering Mr. Nash's walls in the film *A Beautiful Mind*. Mad or not, the result is that I now have a wonderful record of my own journey which I have referred to often, especially while writing this book! Automatic writing is still a part of my daily routine, only I now use my iPad, Apple Pencil and an awesome app called

GoodNotes that turns my iPad into a virtual journal. and save everything electronically. It's still very portable but gives me the added benefit of saving a few trees.

HOMEWORK ASSIGNMENT #18

Automatic Writing Journal Entry

I credit this activity with taking me as far as I did as fast as I did. Try to make this a habit at least 5 days a week. Use my basic meditation or another of your choosing to quiet your mind and tune in, then listen and write for at least 15 minutes. I recommend 30 minutes or more but, once again, doing *something* is one hundred times better than doing *nothing*, so carve out whatever time you can. Remember that I tuned in for two hours every morning before school and countless additional hours after school or two full years before going pro. As with any worthy endeavor, you will get as much out of this as you put into it.

Step 1:

Grab your journal, sit down in your quiet spot and light your candle(s), incense or what have you.

Step 2: Set Your Daily Intention

Do you want to understand yourself or a situation better? Would you like to feel more at peace about something? Do you want to know why something has happened or is happening? Ask your Guides to help you understand whatever it is, or to help you see, feel, know... OR just set an intention based on what you plan to do to better yourself and/or your world. You may choose to write your intention in your journal or to simply say it (aloud or to yourself).

Here's an example that you may find helpful:
"Dear ____, please help me to understand ____, or to become more _____ or less _____, or to see _____, etc. I promise to use whatever knowledge you give me to better myself and/or those around me."

Step 3: Protect, Ground Yourself and Open your Chakras

Read or listen to **Beth's Basic Meditation**, which can be found in writing under Homework Assignment #5 of this book, or on the Psychic Development Resources page of my website: **bethparkermedium.com**.

Step 4: Re-focus and Record

Now that you have raised your vibration and feel connected, re-focus on your intention and record anything that you feel, hear, see or think in your journal. Trust what you "get" and pay attention to the universe throughout the day following this activity. Everyone questions what they receive to some degree when they first begin tuning in. Just listen, scribble down whatever you get and go with it. You will probably start noticing all kinds of "coincidences" throughout the day as well once you get rolling. Remember, these ARE NOT coincidences, they are synchronicity at work... aka the Universe throwing signs your way!

14 CRYSTALS 101

School of Rocks

One psychic booster that I feel is important enough that everyone should have a basic understanding of is crystals. I like to think of crystals as pet rocks with a purpose. This makes me feel less crazy talking to them, which I believe is necessary when activating their energy (which involves humbly asking them to work their magic for you). Many of the people whom I encounter have considered adding crystals to their spiritual repertoire, only to become discouraged or overwhelmed because they have no clue where to begin. There are Lord knows how many species of crystals out there, so I'm going to keep this as simple as I can and give you tips on what I consider to be the basic wardrobe of crystals that you should consider investing in; the little black dresses and cardigans of the rock world. I'll begin with what I believe to be the most useful stones in terms of psychic protection, and then move on to some crystals with chakra balancing properties.

A few words about size, shape and texture. Unless you are

planning on making your crystals do double duty as a bookends or doorstops, this is one time in life where size does not matter. A pebble or palm-sized nugget can be just as useful as a five-pound boulder. Tumbled (smooth), or raw (rough), you ask? There are varying opinions on this subject. Some say they are like most healthy foods, more potent in their natural state, than after having been "processed" (which in this case means tumbled). I have also heard that the less they have been handled during the tumbling and/or packaging process, the less random energy may have been absorbed that could potentially affect its new owner (you). I have a mix of both in my collection and, in my opinion, what matters most is choosing crystals that cry out to you from the box or shelf, as any rescue shelter pet that you might consider adopting would. I have purchased most of my crystals in New Age stores and am primarily attracted by color and shape. Crystals come in a myriad of natural and machine or man-cut shapes. Crystal points and wands are usually favored by those doing Reiki healing and other chakra balancing work. I have been pocketing heart-shaped rocks on my walks for years and, if I am purchasing a crystal and happen across one that is heart-ish shaped (whether raw or tumbled), I consider it a keeper. My daughter and son-in-law are true crystal gurus. They manage to find the most amazing gems out in the wild without even trying, so I'm also quick to use any specimen gifted to me by them.

Beth's Basic Go-To Crystals:
I've mentioned some of my go-to crystals in other blog posts or on social media, but here they are again in a nice little list, followed by my personal picks for each chakra.

Citrine. Golden in color and used to eliminate negative energy, citrine also attracts success and improves digestion. This magical crystal is always at the top of my list and included in every Spirit Party Favor that I give out at readings. If you are a psychic or an empath, you are an energy sponge. A lot of this energy will be retained in your Solar Plexus Chakra, which is at the center of your body, about where your stomach is. Not surprisingly, a lot of empaths suffer from upset or "nervous" stomachs, which is a sign that something is amiss with your third chakra. Using this stone daily when you ground will help to release any negative energy and keep the solar plexus chakra from getting gunked up or fully blocked.

Obsidian and Smokey Quartz. Dark brownish-grey or black in color, both of these "crust busters" absorb negative energy like no other, except maybe amber (which feels like plastic to me, so thanks but no thanks). I hold them to ground myself before meditating or raising my vibration and leave them sitting out at all times for protection from any dark or dank energy that might be lurking about. They are also super low maintenance. Some claim that these stones, like my other fave, citrine, need never be cleansed. I handle mine so often, I've never even needed to dust them like I do the others on occasion.

Selenite. This opaque white stone is a great energy conductor and helps to connect with the higher planes (those mysterious parts of the Universe that can only be seen with the third eye). It has purifying properties as well and is often sold as a stick or wand. You can also purchase a larger flat slab of selenite and use it as a "charging dock" for your other crystals.

Rose Quartz. This light to deep pink crystal is sometimes known as the "romance stone". It helps attract love and to release any negativity associated with heartache, anger or jealousy. I love pink, so I'd keep it around even if it didn't have so many fabulous properties. The downside? it's a bit more high-maintenance than other crystals and needs to be cleansed fairly frequently, especially if you are prone to a lot of drama in your love life.

Regular Garden Variety Rocks ("Psychic Static Busters")
These are, quite literally, rocks that you find in your yard or garden. Years ago, a psychic explained the reason that electronics constantly went hinky on me, and then suggested a solution. Basically, my spazzy energy attracts many other random energies, which then interfere with anything involving an electrical current. His invaluable quick fix? Dig up a palm-sized rock from outside, keep it on my classroom desk and grab it as needed to use as a "circuit grounder". I did as-directed and was amazed by the results. If my phone, laptop or projector froze up, I simply placed one hand on the rock and another on the device. Boom. Problem solved. No more MacBook rainbow wheel of death. If you resist the urge to clean the dirt off of them when you bring them into the house, you can also use these basic rocks to ground when it's too cold or wet to go barefoot outside and connect directly with the earth.

Chakra Stones
There are several crystals or stones associated with each chakra, based on their color and healing properties. The simplest thing to do is go online to Etsy or Amazon, type in "chakra stones" and buy yourself a set. They come rough or tumbled, and some even have pretty chakra symbols printed

on them. If this cheap, mass-produced option does not appeal to you, read on and I will help you to narrow down your choices before you start shopping.

Clear Quartz **(Crown Chakra).** Known as the "master stone" by most, I prefer "Queen of Crystals" because it blows the other peasants away by doing everything they can and more. Healing? Check. Protective? Check. Energizing? Check. Amplifying? Check. You get the picture. Buy some attached to a keychain and consider it kryptonite against any bad juju you encounter when forced to interact with the masses.

Amethyst **(Crown Chakra).** Some people associate this crystal with the Third Eye Chakra, but that leaves out another stone entirely and, as a former teacher, I always try to be as inclusive as possible. Amethyst is light to dark purple and is used to heal any issue or disorder associated with your head or "crown". Put a chunk next to your bed if you are prone to nightmares and ask Violet (the perfect name for this purple pet, no?) to banish the Dark Lords of dreamland.

Lapis Lazuli **(Third Eye Chakra).** This mysterious stone is dark blue, often with specks or veins of gold running through it. It's more expensive than sodalite, so you won't find it any of the chakra stone starter sets, but why skimp on a rock that may open you up to knowledge and visions from other realms? Cleopatra used to grind it up and use it as eyeshadow. If it was good enough for the Cardi B of ancient Egypt, it's good enough for yours truly… Sold!

Angelite **(Throat Chakra).** This is the light blue stone that is skipped over by those who don't put her majesty clear quartz on a throne above the rest of the crystals where she belongs. As the name suggests, it is basically the guardian angel of crystals, offering spiritual protection, healing and inspiration. Open your throat chakra with this stone and you could increase your odds of communicating with the Angels and your Spirit Guides.

Green Aventurine **(Heart Chakra).** Just like that other green harbinger of good luck, the four-leaf clover, this stone is said to bring fortune's blessings. It is sometimes called the gambling stone for this reason and is also useful for opening a blocked Heart Chakra, which helps lower your blood pressure. I recently considered buying an overpriced chunk of this stone on a silver chain from Tiffany's... but I was pretty sure that my doing so would have the opposite effect on my husband's blood pressure.

Citrine **(Solar Plexus Chakra).** I already touted this gem above, so I'll just remind you that if you are reading this, chances are you are an empath (or know one) and *need* to get some to arm yourself against that bully of a boss or moody BFF you've been dealing with for so long.

Carnelian **(Sacral Chakra).** The Sacral Chakra is linked to, among other things, the reproductive organs. I read somewhere that this orange-red stone has the potential to stimulate the metabolism, improve fertility and possibly even reduce frigidity and impotence. It may or may not also help ease the symptoms of menstruation and menopause. I'm seriously considering tucking a pebble of carnelian into the waistband of my underwear to ward off the hot flashes I'm bound to experience as my half-century birthday approaches.

It wouldn't be the first time I was embarrassed by a random rock falling out of my pant leg (doesn't everyone shove a protective crystal in their bra on bad days?)

Red Jasper (**Root Chakra**). The Root Chakra keeps your soul grounded and secure during its journey here on the earthly plane. Red jasper is calming and balances your emotional energy. If you are going through a rough patch or feeling scattered, this might be the spiritual chill pill you've been looking for. Hold some and meditate and you might not need to pop that extra Xanax.

Caring for your New Pet Rocks

As noted above, certain crystals need to be cleansed or recharged more than others. If you are OCD and must be certain that you are caring for them as specified by the crystal police, please go directly to Mr. Google and take copious notes on how to best nurture each. Generally speaking, the more you use a crystal, the more frequently it needs a "bath" of some sort. There are several methods for cleansing or recharging crystals. I will share three below. Read them and choose the one that suits you and your pet rocks best.

Full Moon Recharge

This is exactly what it sounds like. Rinse your crystals and then take them outside or arrange them on a windowsill overnight to bask in the glow of the full moon. I fall asleep early and can barely manage to brush my teeth before bedtime, so this happens a few times a year at most chez-moi.

Dirt Bath

Go outside, dig a hole and bury your crystals for at least 24 hours. Extra time in the ground won't hurt them, just be sure to remember where you buried them before Fido goes digging and chokes on one. Rinse off the dirt and you're good to go.

Salt Spa Treatment
Grab a bowl and enough sea salt or (my fave) pink himalayan salt to cover your crystals. Bury them and let them relax and recharge for at least 24 hours. Rinse the salt off and voilà, your stone servants are rejuvenated and ready to serve you once more. Be sure to chuck the used salt. This may seem wasteful to you thrifty types, but consuming the salt that just absorbed all that negative energy kinda defeats the purpose, am I right?

A final note on the magic of crystals. In the words of George Michael, "You gotta have faith, faith, faith". In other words, they are only as powerful as you believe them to be, so try to suspend any doubt that you might be harboring, and they might just rock your world (pun intended).

HOMEWORK ASSIGNMENT #19

Adopt Your First Pet Rock

You need not spend a lot (or any) money on this assignment. The purpose of this is to introduce you to the magical healing and grounding properties of crystals.

Head outside to your backyard or to the nearest New Age store. If you are in a store, browse the crystals, picking up any that you are drawn to.

Check them out from every angle. Hold them in the palm of your hand and then close your hand around them to feel how they "fit". Just as some people love big slobbery dogs and others prefer small "cat-dogs", so might you prefer one pet rock over another. Choose the one that you like the best based on color, shape or size (the reason doesn't matter). If you have chosen to seek out a more feral rock from the yard, dig up a few and follow the same selection process.

1. *Energize your new pet by giving it a bath. A quick rinse under the tap is sufficient.*

2. *Activate (train) your rock by holding it in your hand, telling it how you intend to use it and asking it to enhance your life with its magical properties.*

15 TAROT 101

Divination Tools for Beginners

Remember those paper cootie catchers that you made back in grade school? How about the ubiquitous Magic Eight Ball? Divination tools are anything that is used to predict the future and there are thousands of them out there. We are hardwired and socialized to be practical, rational and use our brains to think everything through. These tools help us to bypass our intellect (stop thinking) and access our intuition, that inner voice that guides us via our gut instincts and feelings. I've dabbled a bit with several divination tools (rune stones, tea leaves and palmistry to name a few), but I've been reading Tarot cards for decades and I think they are a great way to hone your skills. On my 18th birthday my parents got me a hope chest and an introductory Tarot kit which included a deck of cards, a black cloth with the Celtic Cross layout printed on it, and a how-to book. Thirty-plus years (and a gazillion readings) later, I no longer use that first set, but it is safely tucked away amongst my other treasured mementos in the behemoth wooden chest. Having graduated from amateur card reader to professional psychic medium, I no longer use any actual cards during readings, but what I learned from them has proven invaluable, and my Guides frequently use them as a tool to give me insight. For example, more often than not, before a client even arrives for a reading, I will be shown the first and second cards that they would have drawn, which allows me to quickly understand what he or she might need guidance about or what our focus will be.

When I began reading the cards all those years ago, I was eager to dive in but didn't have the foggiest idea of where to begin interpreting each card individually (let alone in combination with any of the other seventy-seven in the deck), so I would simply lay out the ten cards chosen and refer back to the book as I turned each one over. While this did help me to learn each card's meanings, at some point it became a bit tiresome (largely due to the stilted old school language of that first how-to book, which was full of words like *augurs*, *portends* and *concretize*), so I struck out on a more intuitive approach as I became more confident in my skills. Whether or not you fall in love with the Tarot like I did, I think it is a great tool that can help you tap into your intuition, as well as introduce you to the fascinating world of divination.

Choosing a Tarot Deck
So many decks, so little time. There is an endless array of beguiling decks from which to choose. I myself have bought or been gifted a dozen or more over the years, featuring everything from witches and fairies to Tahitian totems. Each deck generally comes with its own instruction manual (some

even have each card's meaning printed right on them), but you'll want to have at least one solid book on hand for reference. Almost every book out there on the subject works with the Rider Waite Tarot (aka "Rider Waite Smith" or "Waite Smith"), so unless you positively cannot fathom using a deck of cards featuring anything other than the cast of the Lord of the Rings, I suggest starting with a deck by that name or with the word "universal" featured in the title. If the deck does not come with a book or instructional pamphlet which includes a basic ten card spread, you will want to purchase a how-to book that includes at least a few sample spreads, which are usually found towards the back as an ancillary.

Choosing a Spread
There are nearly as many spreads to choose from as there are fancy card decks. As someone who likes to keep things as simple as possible (and as the mother of an indecisive Libra who has learned to narrow down the choices), I suggest that you stick to the ever-popular ten-card Celtic Cross or another basic ten-card spread until you get the hang of things. I have used several spreads over the years, but I always come back to three that work best for my purposes: the aforementioned Celtic Cross, a follow-up spread that I call "Cut-the-Deck-into-3-Piles-for-your-Past/Present/Future" and, if further clarification is needed, a five or seven card "Horseshoe" spread.

Preparing a Card Reading and Interpreting the Spread
Some people refuse to let anyone else touch or handle their sacred Tarot deck, but I had no such qualms. I kept my cards in a small red silk purse and would never let anyone else play around with or handle them unnecessarily but, being neither

superstitious nor a germaphobe, I have always allow the sitter to shuffle the deck because I feel it is helpful to get their vibes involved. You will quickly notice that most Tarot cards are larger than those found in a standard deck, and most people feel a bit clumsy with them. None of that matters. Just have them "schmuffle" the cards about to the best of their ability. Lay the cards out according to whatever instructions you are following. Remember that where each card falls in the spread is as important as which card falls there.

The Minor Arcana
Most people don't realize that the Tarot deck is just a fancy deck of playing cards with twenty-two bonus cards (aka the Major Arcana) thrown in to spice things up. The Minor Arcana is made up of fifty-six cards in four suits. The cards with Pentacles (sometimes called "coins") are your diamonds, the Swords are spades, the Wands are clubs, and the Cups are hearts. Each tarot suit includes an Ace, cards numbered two through ten, a Knight, Queen and King, plus an extra Page or "Knave" (a Joker, if you will); which is why there are fifty-six basic cards, instead of the usual fifty-two. Your instruction manual will probably go into great detail about the meaning of each card or grouping of cards, but it's important not to get too mired in the minutiae and to be sure to take note of the bigger picture as soon as the cards are laid out. This will allow you to begin relying on your intuition from the start, using the book on an as-needed basis, or as a part-time crutch, rather than a full-time wheelchair.

Each of the four suits is also ruled by an element and associated with a particular arena of life. Cups are ruled by Water and associated with emotions. Swords fall under the influence of

Air and are indicators of mental activity and/or health issues. Pentacles relate to the element of Earth and are associated with money and finances. Wands fall under the element of Fire and represent growth, work and creative pursuits. As I noted earlier, before you start analyzing each individual card it is important to look at the spread as a whole. Are there a lot of cards with Cups on them? If so, the reading will be focused on relationships, love and matters of the heart. If Pentacles pop up throughout, someone has money on their mind. A preponderance of Wands usually means personal growth or work will figure prominently, and an abundance of Swords could indicate a lot of mental pressure or stress in someone's life. The court cards (King, Queen, Knight and Page) can sometimes represent a situation, but more often than not represent the person you are reading for or someone in their life. Depending on the person's age, Kings and Queens might represent a father, mother, husband or wife. Pages represent a younger person (a child, sibling or friend of the sitter). Knights (in shining armor or otherwise) often pop up in a romantic reading.

The Major Arcana
There are roughly half as many cards in the Major Arcana, yet they purportedly have far greater influence in a reading. These are often referred to as the fate cards and, thanks to the strong imagery, tend to be the cards that freak people out when they appear. I can always count on a gasp of horror when the Tower —which features people diving out of the windows as it to be bursts into flame— turns up in a spread. The Empress, on the other hand, features a voluptuous, motherly figure and therefore only frightens those who have some prior knowledge of the cards, like my daughters and their friends who always

cringed as teenagers when she popped up because they knew this might indicate that someone was knocked up (or would be soon). The Empress can, however, also indicate an issue with one's mother. Every card has at least two meanings, which is why you must always pay attention to the surrounding cards. Some people get pale or start sweating when they see the Devil or Death cards, but unless they are next to each other and/or accompanied by the nine or ten of Swords, they are not a bad omen. The Death card usually just symbolizes the end of something, often an outdated way of thinking or being, which is necessary to achieve growth. The Devil, which in most decks features two people chained together, is actually quite favorable when associated with marriage because it symbolizes a strong or unbreakable bond (a happy spin on the proverbial ball and chain). Helpful hint: one of the ways that I memorized the meanings of these key cards was to go over each of them in my mind, in lieu of counting sheep, any time that I had trouble falling asleep.

A note on reversals (cards that are upside down in a spread): by and large these are portrayed as having an opposite or ominous/negative aspect of the upright meaning of a card. I don't personally go for that line of thinking. I also feel there's enough to learn about the upright meanings when you are first starting out, so my advice is to flip them all right side up as you lay them out, at least until you have a good grasp on the original meanings.

How often should I read my own cards, or read for others?
Read your own cards as often as you want. Everyone gets a little card happy when they are getting started, because it's the easiest way to practice. As far as reading for others goes, my

general rule of thumb has always been to wait at least three months between spreads. There are two reasons for this. First, you want to give it enough time for things to play out and to let knew situations develop. Second, it discourages your friends and family from becoming as addicted to the readings as you may be at first. There's no need to start an all-out Tarot Zombie Apocalypse, am I right? A final word of warning before you tiptoe into the wonderful world of Tarot. Please do not read too much into, or rely too heavily on the cards, especially if you are reading your own six times a day for practice. Always keep in mind that, ultimately, the decisions that influence fate and destiny rest in your own hands, not in the cards. Treat them as a tool which can help you to hone your intuition and thoughtfully guide your actions and they will serve you well… and be less likely to become a weapon of mental mass destruction that controls your every action. I would also caution you against offering your services for pay too soon. Getting to that level takes a lot of time and practice, so be prepared to work for it.

HOMEWORK ASSIGNMENT #20

Hone Your Intuition with the Tarot

This assignment will require you to purchase a set of tarot cards, which are relatively inexpensive. A reference book is handy, but if you're not ready to make that kind of financial commitment, you can use the internet and choose option two below.

Option 1

For those readers who were especially inspired by my intro to Tarot and plan to take full advantage of this tool:

- *Purchase a Tarot starter set which includes a deck and how-to book, or a set of cards and a separate reference book of your choosing.*

- *Find the basic ten-card spread and instructions included.*

- *Shuffle the cards, choose ten, and lay them out according to the instructions.*

- *Look at the spread holistically. Make note of any patterns that you see. Are there more of one suit than any other, lots of face cards that represent people, or several cards from the major arcana present? Make a note of these findings in your journal.*

- *Look at each card individually without opening your book. What do you intuitively feel each card might represent or mean? Jot down whatever comes to mind for each card.*

- *Now open your book and look up each card individually. How do your impressions match up with the book's description? Don't worry about how close or far apart you were from the book. I suspect you will find at least a few similarities, but the important thing is that you are relying on your own inner psychic to begin reading the cards intuitively, while also gaining some insights — for future reference— from the book.*

- *Finally, take a look at each card in terms of position. Following the spread instructions, jot down any impressions you get about the relevance of why each card may have popped up in particular position.*

Option 2

This activity is designed for those of you who aren't interested in doing full readings for yourself or others, or as an extra credit assignment for the Tarot buffs who chose option 1:

- *Purchase a basic set of Universal Tarot cards.*

- *Shuffle the cards and then cut the deck into three piles.*

- *The left pile represents the past, the middle is the present and the right is the future.*

- *Think about what has gone on recently in your life.*

- *Flip the top card from each pile and jot down what you intuitively feel each might mean or represent based on what has happened recently, what is going on now, and what could potentially happen.*

- *Find a free online Tarot resource and look up the meaning of each card that you drew. How did your interpretation compare to what you read online? What insights can you gather from this?*

- *If you'd like to clarify or explore any of the piles (past, present or future) further, flip another card or two from each pile and repeat the process.*

16 PSYCHIC CIRCLES AND PARTNER ACTIVITIES

Sometimes More Is Merrier

As a student I loathed group projects and as a teacher I tried only to assign them if I thought the work would easier or more fun to do in a group. I love teaching groups and holding small psychic development circles, however, because everyone gets to focus on their own development while simultaneously learning from the experiences of others. This book is pretty much geared towards those homebodies like me who prefer exercising alone in the basement to a spandex-filled meat market (aka gym), but if you can round up a few kindred spirits, I think you'll have fun and gain a lot from the final five homework assignments.

You will need one person to take charge and organize your circle, but they need not be an expert or fully developed psychic. I didn't have to look very far to find willing participants for my first development circle. They pretty much fell into my lap in the form of three seniors from the high school I was teaching in, plus my youngest daughter who was eager to join. Out of respect for the varied religious beliefs of my students and their families —and the potential for some of them to be frightened or freaked out by the news— I did not openly share the fact that I was a psychic medium with all of my classes. I did, however, share it with my Senior Student Aide, Emily, who (*not* coincidentally) turned out to be a born medium. I also shared it with the students who had lost parents so that I could help them to heal by delivering messages. Even then (no matter *how* persistent the deceased parent was) I was careful to make sure that the student was ready, and to let the living parent know in case they had any objections. In any event, Emily and a few of her girlfriends became obsessed with all things psychic and, before long, I suggested that we form a psychic circle so that they could begin to understand how it works and raise their own intuition. I created a lesson plan and activities for each meeting just as I would for any other class that I taught, many of which were the basis for the assignments in this book. I consider all of the activities here to be tried and true because I have successfully used them in both private mentoring sessions and psychic development circles. Just as you need not be psychic to lead a group, you also need not be a teacher. You've got everything you need in this book to get a circle going. Put sticky notes on the pages containing any assignments or activities that you want to use during any given circle meeting, gather enough pens and paper to go around, and you're ready to roll!

Everyone that I have worked with thus far has been able to connect with the Universe in a way that they previously had not, with some showing a greater degree of natural ability than others. The same will be true with any circle that you find yourself a part of, so the most important thing is that you choose a group of people who will encourage and support one another. I'm all about inclusivity in education, but if you know someone who might be interested, but you also know them to have a less-than-positive attitude or feel that their energy would not mesh with the others involved, find someone else. Everyone should have an open mind and be excited about it. A development circle is *not* the place to be convincing or converting skeptics. In general, I have found that each person benefits the most and gets better results in a small group that makes them feel secure and connected rather than in a large, more impersonal assembly. It is also much easier to get three to six people to fully commit to meeting on a regular basis, and to work out a scheduled day and time.

Whether or not you create an organized development circle, I highly encourage you to find at least one friend (or rope in your significant other) so that you can take advantage of the following activities which require a minimum of two living bodies.

HOMEWORK ASSIGNMENT #21

Psychometry

Psychometry is the ability to read a person's energy by holding an object that belonged to them. Metal and cloth hold energy better than most materials, so his activity works best if you use items such as jewelry, keys, clothing, or anything that the person touched, used or wore often.

I believe that you will get the most out of this activity by having everyone involved listen to my basic meditation —found on the *Psychic Development Resources* page of my website, **bethparkermedium.com**— or any other similar meditation that you have found or created for the same purpose. At the very least, you should have everyone close their eyes, and lead them through three to four deep breaths, inhaling positive thoughts and energy and exhaling any negative thoughts or energy. If it is just you and one other person who is game enough to go along but doesn't want to actively participate, procure an object from them, follow the directions and then confer again with them afterwards for validation of your impressions.

- *Open your journal(s) to a blank page.*

- *Swap objects (everyone should be working with an object other than their own).*

- *Open your mind and chakras with meditation or deep breathing as suggested above.*

- *Once everyone feels tuned in, start jotting any and everything that you see, hear or feel as you hold the object. Male/female, colors, numbers, names, images, sensations... literally anything that pops into your mind's eye (or ear) uninvited. Try your best not to second guess or judge your impressions.*
- *Share what you got. Applaud and encourage any "hits", be they big or small, rather than trying to explain away near-misses.*

HOMEWORK ASSIGNMENT #22

Reading Photographs

This is the same basic activity as psychometry, only you will be using photographs in lieu of objects. The subject of the photograph can be an animal or a human, living or deceased. Each participant should use a photograph of someone that they know anything about. You can even have the entire group read each photograph, with the person who provided the photo sitting out that round until it is time to provide validation.

I believe that you will get the most out of this activity by having everyone involved listen to my basic meditation —found on the *Psychic Development Resources* page of my website, **bethparkermedium.com**— or any other similar meditation that you have found or created for the same purpose. At the very least, you should have everyone close their eyes, and lead them through three to four deep breaths, inhaling positive thoughts and energy and exhaling any negative thoughts or energy. If it is just you and one other person who is game enough to go along but doesn't want to actively participate, procure a photograph from them, follow the directions and then confer again with them afterwards for validation of your impressions.

- *Open your journal(s) to a blank page.*

- *Swap photos (everyone should be working with a photo other than their own). I suggest starting with the photos face up because this is much less intimidating. As you gain more confidence, you try it with the photo(s) face down.*

- *Open your mind and chakras with meditation or deep breathing as suggested above.*

- *Once everyone feels tuned in, start jotting down any and everything that you see, hear or feel as you hold the photo. Male/female, colors, names, ages, birthday months, numbers, names, images, sensations... literally anything that pops into your mind's eye (or ear) uninvited. Try your best not to second guess or judge your impressions.*

- *Share what you got. Applaud and encourage any "hits", be they big or small. It is important to remain flexible and look for possible connections rather than trying to minimize or explain away things that aren't an exact fit.*

HOMEWORK ASSIGNMENT #23

Telepathy

My husband could probably explain this even better than I can because I've been subjecting him to these little practice sessions ever since I discovered my gift. I'm going to give a few suggestions, starting with the most basic to help you get warmed up and more relaxed about the process. As always, I think it is best to start with a meditation or a few deep calming breaths, but you can practice these less formally any time or place (to pass the time in the car on a long drive, or while sitting on the beach, for example).

- *If you are in a more formal circle setting, have each pair of people sit back to back.*

- *Have everyone involved listen to my basic meditation —found on the Psychic Development Resources page of my website,* **bethparkermedium.com**— *or any other similar meditation that you have found or created for the same purpose. At the very least, you should have everyone close their eyes, and lead them through three to four deep breaths, inhaling positive thoughts and energy and exhaling any negative thoughts or energy. If it is just you and one other person who is game enough to go along but has no interest in being a human Zoltar, just ask them to do the thinking while you stick to playing the role of the mind reader.*

- *Take turns being the transmitter/receiver. Ask one person to think of something specific. Start with something simple like a shape, color or number between one and thirty. Make sure that the transmitter holds that one specific thought until the receiver has come up with a response. Animals, foods and household objects are also good subjects.*

- *Step it up a notch the next go round and have them focus on a specific emotion. If they are able to come up with an incident that* they associate with that emotion, ask them to focus on that memory. It's really cool when someone picks up on not only the emotion, but a detail or two tied to the memory!

- Applaud and encourage any "hits", be they big or small. It is important to remain flexible and look for possible connections rather than try to minimize or explain away things that aren't an exact fit. I once casually asked my husband to guess what I was thinking about and he came up with a "white square". I had been thinking about the pee pad that I had forgotten to put down for our dog... which is in fact a white square!

This is the simplest of activities and the possibilities are endless. If you can conjure up an image, you're good to go. The only time you may run into trouble is if you are dealing with someone who has Aphantasia, which is the inability to *see* things when imagining them. I can't begin wrap my head around this handicap, but apparently there are plenty of peeps out there who cannot summon a lifelike image of something real or imaginary.

HOMEWORK ASSIGNMENT #24

Partner Aura Reading

This activity will probably take a bit of prep work. Unless everyone is super comfortable checking their Chakras for any wobbly wheels, you will need to do a bit of research ahead and find an online Chakra test, or head to the *Psychic Development Page* of my website, **bethparkermedium.com**, and click on the **Online Chakra Quiz** link provided.

- *Find a Chakra test or quiz online and share the link with everyone who is participating.*

- *Make sure that no one shares their results with anyone else.*

- *Either partner up and take turns reading each other's auras, or have the whole group read one person at a time.*

- *Prepare by having everyone listen to my basic meditation, found on the* **Psychic Development Resources** *page of my website,* **bethparkermedium.com**.

- *Focus on the person whose aura you are reading. If you are a natural at aura reading (if you can squint or blur your eyes and see the colors surrounding a person), go to it and write down the first or dominant color that you see. List any other colors or layers that you see as well.*

- *If you are not able to do this, focus on the person and then imagine a white screen behind them. Picture a vertical string of seven balls of light behind them, starting with purple at the top of their head, followed by indigo, light blue, green, yellow, orange, and red at the bottom. Scan each of these seven colors and look for any "flashing lights" or other aberrations that set them apart from the others, which indicates a problem area. Make a note of the color or colors that seemed "off".*

- *Share what you got and see how closely it matches the results of the chakra test. Don't get upset if you feel like you failed this homework assignment. Aura reading can be tricky and, just like with the other activities, there are usually one or two people who are naturally better at it than the rest.*

HOMEWORK ASSIGNMENT #25

Reading the Energy of a Space (Field Trip!)

Just as people and objects have energy that can be read, so do locations. I love doing this and spent a lot of time doing it when I moved into my husband's neighborhood because he had lived there long enough to know a lot about what had happened where, but I had never stepped foot in his neck of the woods prior to meeting him. He'd point to a house and I would tune in and go, "Suicide in the garage. I can't breathe, so hanging or asphyxiation?", and I was always pretty much on target. There's an historic section that goes back to the 16 and 1700s, so I would sometimes pick up on things that he couldn't validate, but I still considered it good practice. We do this on vacation as well. He'll research and get the 4-1-1 on famous haunted locations, but keep it secret from me. Then when we visit, I fill him in on what I get, and he's able to confirm whether or not I'm on the mark.

- *One person in the pair or group needs to have background knowledge of the place you are visiting ahead of time. Be sure to tell them not to share any details.*

- *If it's a neighborhood, keep walking until you either sense some new energy or they tell you to focus on a specific house or location.*

- *Quiet your mind and tune in to the energy and report anything that you see, hear or feel. You might see specifics having to do with people or events tied to the location, or just get an overwhelming feeling like, "Yuck! Let's get out of here!"*

- *Share your impressions and see if anything matches up with what is known about the place.*

17 RELATIONSHIPS

Another Important Psychic P.S.A.

The Spirit World can be all-consuming, particularly if it turns into a career, so be prepared for it to affect your personal relationships. It takes a very special person to live with a psychic. I have sung the praises of my husband throughout this book because, quite honestly, he calms my crazy and keeps me grounded in a way that neither a mountain of citrine nor all of the sand in our backyard beach ever could. When we were matched online and his profile popped up, he was so totally my type that I feared he was too good to be true. Fortunately, he was even better in person than his online dating profile had promised. It was as if I had ordered up my favorite Chick-fil-a meal: "I'll take a number one, tall, with salt and pepper hair and side of great legs". It is no coincidence that my own awakening coincided with the best relationship decision I have ever made, which was choosing him. From the moment we met I was instantly comfortable and at ease, and anytime I was at his house I felt as if I was on vacation, despite his pesky house ghost. I had been married twice before though and was wary of making the same (or new) mistakes again and he was a confirmed bachelor. Basically, before we met he had said "Never" and I had said "Never again", yet three years later we found ourselves saying "I do" twice; once, unofficially, during a romantic trip to Bora Bora and then again, officially, a few weeks later in front of our families. As soon as I recognized the magnitude of the gift that I had been given I instinctively knew that anything (or anyone) who disapproved or stood in the way would have to go. The fact that he stuck by me through my spiritual metamorphosis tells you everything you need to know about why he made the cut. The moral here? If you must be with someone, be with someone who believes in you as much or more than you believe in yourself. If, with the help of this book or by some other means, you recognize that your gift is similar to mine and you are truly invested in devoting your life to The Spirit World, my advice is to go find yourself a Scott or be prepared to go it alone.

You may find yourself reevaluating your non-romantic relationships as well. I was, again, fortunate enough to have a very loving and supportive group of friends, especially my VBTFs (very best teacher friends), Michelle, Lisa, Marisa, and Aimee. Sure, they may have been a little freaked out at first, but I was always the crazy one among our crew, so they probably weren't as shocked as they would have been had it been Michelle —the most practical and least flaky among us—— who turned up one day talking to everyone's dead people. They not only accepted it, however, they embraced it and encouraged me. Michelle, who lives in the community where we taught, believed in me enough to go out on a limb and host my first official group reading, which included the parents of some of our students. I'm sure there were plenty of people around the school who either didn't believe or thought I'd lost my damn mind when I announced that I was retiring to take up my new trade full-time, but I've never been one to give a fiddler's fart what other people think, which made me a perfect candidate for this job. Being comfortable enough to approach the stranger next you on a plane or in line at the supermarket and ask them about their departed family or friends who happen to drop in from the Spirit World is pretty much a prerequisite of this career as well.

Not everyone in your life will be totally thrilled or on board with your new reality. Some people resist change and will need a little more time getting used to the new you. One of my daughters is wired the same way that I am and was almost as excited about my newfound gift as I was from the get-go. Given our shared experiences, the family has voted her most likely to follow in my funky footsteps. The other is a calmer, more practical individual so it took her a little time to warm up to the idea. This was very understandable. Most kids would be a bit unsettled to find out that their mom was suddenly psychic. Other family members were a little creeped out by the whole idea. I tried my best not to shove it down anyone's throat and to respect the fact that an adjustment period was in order for some. I encourage you to do the same when confronted with any hesitation or straight up opposition that you may encounter from your nearest and dearest. My daughter finally came around to the point that she now uses her amazing organizational skills to manage and keep track of my larger events, but my brother may never be able to wrap his head around the fact that I gave up a perfectly solid job and a pension to talk to dead people. I'm fine with this. Aside from being personable and outgoing people, Rex and I could not be more opposite. Just as he took after my mom's Italian family who tans easily and I take after the pasty Irish on my dad's side, so too did he inherit my mom's "if I can't see it, I don't believe it" attitude. Reality is ninety percent perception and our perceptions have often been ninety degrees apart since childhood. We still love each other —how could I not love the boy who kept me safe in the dark as a kid and the man who took care of our mom after our dad died— and we find it quite easy to agree to disagree. I'd be lying, however, if I said that I don't look forward to the day when he comes to me from the Other Side and I get to stick my tongue out at him and say, "Told ya so, butt head!" As for other skeptics, I always tell people to bring them along. I never feel any added pressure to convince them. I don't care about or concern myself with changing their minds because if I did, I would lose focus on what matters, receiving and delivering healing messages for those who need them.

18 BUMPS IN THE ROAD

Managing Mindset and Expectations

Nothing was more magical —and truly life changing— than the moment I realized my first few experiences communicating with the Other Side weren't just flukes; that I was actually legitimately, totally psychic. I felt, and still feel, like I won the Lifepath Lottery. My new connection to the Spiritnet put everything in perspective and completely changed the way I think about and view things forever, and I suspect it will do the same for you should you find yourself in my shoes. Richard Carlson's credo, "Don't sweat the small stuff… and it's all small stuff," suddenly made more sense than ever, and I was able to see how trivial and unnecessary most of our First World Probs truly are. As with every path or highway in life, however, there are a few pitfalls or potholes that you need to be aware of and prepared to dodge when possible. I addressed many of these perils in Part II of this book, which dealt with the do's and don'ts of staying sane as a psychic, but I want to take a moment to focus a bit more on mindset and expectations; both your own and those of others.

Although I can't imagine the happy honeymoon period that follows a true intuitive awakening ever completely vanishing or leading to a nasty divorce from Spirit, there will be times where frustration sets in and the struggle is real. At times you may feel like you can't get rid of a certain "static" on your Spirit Station, or that there are messages that you just don't "get". Figuring out why something is happening and how to correct it can sometimes feel like trying to solve an expert level Sudoku puzzle. It can be even more maddening when you take it to your Spirit Guides, and they seem less than keen to offer up an easy solution. Fear not. They haven't abandoned you. I have found that this simply means that the lesson I am meant to learn from the current challenge is more important than most and will be worth the wait (and nails destroyed due to biting them in angst). When this happens to me —Yes! It still happens because one never stops learning— I write down everything that I *do* get from my Guides during my morning meditation, re-read it for any hidden clues I may have missed and, if all else fails, seek out advice from another trusted medium. During the first two years of my development I paid for a few mentoring sessions with the trusted psychic that I mentioned earlier. I wasn't looking for a full reading, however, just some tutoring and this was quite costly. Recognizing that others may find themselves in the same boat, I now offer private psychic tutoring sessions to serious students (those who have taken the time to read this book, for starters) at a reasonable rate (not much more than I would charge to tutor someone in French). These sessions are *not* readings. They are hour long one-on-one Q&A sessions aimed at helping you get over any humps in your development. For more information on this service, as well as the others that I provide, visit the *Psychic Development Resources* page of my website, **bethparkermedium.com**.

Allow me to offer a couple of pieces of advice while we are on the subject of money. I offered up my services as often as I possibly could for free for about a year and a half before I began accepting paying clients. To be honest, I had a very difficult time charging at all, and at the very beginning I feared that if I did, my gift would be taken away. As with most professions, how much you charge will increase with experience. I was so anxious and pressed about how much or how little to charge that my Guides threw up their hands one morning and offered up a simple (and loud!) solution: charge the first fifty clients fifty dollars, the next seventy-five people seventy-five, then one hundred... and go from there. I went up and down and back and forth a bit on this for a while because I found that I usually spent far more than the allotted hour with each client, but I still think this was very sage advice and helped me to relax about the whole money issue. If anyone makes you feel guilty about charging "too much", remember that most women are willing to spend a hundred bucks or more each month on their hair, nails and such. The moment I heard how much people are willing to pay to install and maintain their fake eyelashes or to make sure that their eyebrows are "on fleek" was a game changer for me. If someone doesn't flinch about spending ninety dollars to look like Tammy Faye Baker but they balk at paying to hear from their dearly departed, that's their problem, not mine. I happily donate readings to silent auctions for charities and provide many readings free of charge for other reasons. I doubt that those who inject face fillers to fix crow's feet can say the same. Just sayin'. We are all a part of the service industry and, sacred though your gift may be, you deserve to get paid for the service you are providing. I can assure you of two things; Spirit does not want you to become a starving psychic and, if you get to the point of hanging a psychic shingle above the door, if you are fully developed and prepared, clients will line up fairly quickly.

Early on in my career as a professional medium it became clear to me that there was a huge range of expectations among everyone who came for a reading. Although I always do my very best and, nine times out of ten, walk away feeling like a client's loved ones and my Spirit Guides have knocked it out of the park, how satisfied they are depends greatly on the expectations that they have before they walk in the door. Someone's deceased father will name just about every single family member alive or dead (including pets), followed by a dozen other spot-on validations, but if he doesn't give them the one specific detail that they requested (usually something along the lines of "Where'd you hide the money?"), they throw the proverbial baby out with the bathwater and walk away disappointed. This used to really wear on me, not for myself, but for the loving souls who had worked so hard to communicate in order to validate their continued presence in little Susie's life. I'm an extrovert and enjoy talking to anyone (dead or alive). Aside from the odd pedo or pervert who comes through with an apology, I'm going to enjoy the company and convo regardless. Dear old dad, on the other hand, was busting his butt up there —and doing a bang-up job— but his daughter's mindset got in the way of what should have been a spectacular reunion. In response to this issue, I wrote an extensive blog post, *What to Expect from a Reading: Aligning Expectation with Reality*, and created an entire page devoted to what to expect on my website. I send every new client the links to both and encourage them to do their homework before their scheduled appointment. These resources explain how I communicate with Spirit and (because no two mediums are exactly the same) help clients to understand how their experience with me may be different from what they've seen on TV. I feel it is also imperative that people know that I don't have anyone Up There on speed dial and have no say in who does or doesn't come through during a reading. If a medium asks who you are hoping to hear from ahead of time, guarantees who will come through, or promises that all of your questions will be answered, big red flags should go up in your mind because they might be a fraud. On occasion I encounter someone on the Other Side —usually a parent— who *insists* that I let the client know that they will show up on the appointed day, but I usually just get a mini "preview" of who will be visiting from the Spirit World right before the reading takes place. More often than not the person they are hoping to hear from shows up, but I can't (and won't) say one hundred percent for sure until we get down to business. I'm not in charge of who makes an appearance, Spirit is, and if unexpected rather than expected guests pop in, there is always a reason. I have complete faith in this and often quote the Rolling Stones to get my point across, "You can't always get what you want, but you get what you need." I'm all about working smarter as opposed to harder, by the way, so feel free to share the resources mentioned above with your own prospective clients or use them as an example if you decide to create something similar. The "What to Expect" page can be found on my website, **bethparkermedium.com**, and the blog post can be found online here: **bethparkermedium.blogspot.com**. The Forever Family Foundation has also put together a very nice "What to Expect" pamphlet for those who seek a reading with their certified mediums. This can be found on their website (www.foreverfamilyfoundation.org).

19 WHAT COMES NEXT

Continuing Your Educational Journey

Many of my clients ask how I came so far so quickly as a psychic medium. My answer to this is always, "Hard work and dedication. Once I realized what was happening, I threw myself into it and never looked back." I think the fact that I was a teacher, as were my Spirit Guides when they were here on Earth, helped a lot as well. The next question, especially if they have had psychic or paranormal experiences, is how they themselves can take it to the next level. My answer to this second question is again, "Hard work and dedication." While I believe that some people are born mediums, I am positive that everyone has some degree of intuitive or psychic potential which can be tapped and developed in order to benefit themselves and others.

What else can you do to help the learning process along once you've read this and completed all of the homework assignments? Read and watch anything you can get your hands-on involving psychics and mediums. Instead of a Psychic

Development Circle you could form a Psychic Book Club that meets monthly. I've prepared a list of what I consider to be must-read books for understanding yourself and how the universe works in order to develop your intuitive and psychic gifts, so you could start off by having everyone read — shameless plug— this book and go down the list from there. I consider each of the psychic authors included to have been my own at-home tutors, but I could not finish this book without paying special homage to the woman whom I consider to be the Rock Star of Mediums, Kim Russo. I don't get star-struck around other celebrities —not even the few who have popped in from the Spirit World during readings— but I could barely contain my excitement when I met my idol in the flesh at a Forever Family Foundation event. I even got up the nerve to approach her bodyguard son and ask for a picture with her. I was a super fan of Kim's show *The Haunting Of...* long before I had recognized my own gifts. Once I did, my Guides took full advantage and turned every episode into what can best be described as a distance learning class. I watched and re-watched them with my new psychic lens and my Guides would find a way to help me apply my new knowledge in some way shortly afterwards. If you've seen it, you know that Kim does a fantastic job of explaining her process every step of the way, and there is not a single nugget of wisdom imparted that I haven't used since going pro. While I appreciate all of the other programs out there featuring mediums and how much they have done to create a greater acceptance of our craft, I relate best to Kim's style. Every paranormal investigation that I do flows very much like an episode of her show, with a mixed bag of loving and protective deceased family members and perhaps not-so-welcome Spirits chiming in throughout the course of the day. I haven't yet had the chance to read her new book,

Your Soul Purpose, but I can't wait to get my hands on it. If this book helps even one person as much as Kim's first book and TV show helped me to unleash my inner psychic, I will be honored… and doing cartwheels!

The goal of the time that we spend both here on the earthly plane, as well as on the Other Side between lives, is to learn the lessons that help our souls evolve to higher planes of consciousness. Light Workers —psychics, mediums, intuitive life coaches and the like— are tasked with helping others to achieve this goal. I believe that all teachers are Light Workers as well, and I feel beyond blessed to get to combine my two careers to bring as much awareness of the light and love that exists in the Universe as I possibly can. My hope as a teacher and medium authoring this book is that it helps you to excavate and bring forth the light and wisdom that is your birthright, allowing you to connect to a higher state of consciousness and the divinity within, so that you might one day be compelled to do the same for others.

To learn more about mediumship, the services that I offer or to access the development tools discussed in this book, visit my website: **bethparkermedium.com**

Follow me on Facebook or Instagram:
@bethparkermedium

Beth's Top 10 DIY Psychic Development Booklist:

Infinite Quest by John Edward

Practical Praying by John Edward

Wisdom from Your Spirit Guides by James Van Praagh

The Happy Medium by Kim Russo

Many Lives, Many Masters by Brian Weiss

Angel Intuition by Tanya Carroll Richardson

Everyday Psychic Defense by Cassandra Eason

The Book of Psychic Symbols by Melanie Barnum

Crystal Healing and the Human Energy Field by Marion McGeough

The Smudging and Blessings Book by Jane Alexander

READER NOTES

READER NOTES

Made in United States
North Haven, CT
27 February 2023

33256600R00107